Public Housing Resident to Seminary President: A Pastor's Memoir

R. Robert Cueni

LUCAS PARK BOOKS

ST. LOUIS, MISSOURI

The following have given permission to use material in this book:
Two Sisters Photography, Ludington, Michigan, for the use of Cueni family photo.

Christian Board of Publication, Saint Louis, Missouri, *The Disciple* magazine, July 16, 1978, for the use of the poem, "It All Depends."

ISBN: 978-1-60350-031-9

Published by Lucas Park Books
www.lucasparkbooks.com

Printed in the United States of America

Contents

Preface iv

1 First Steps down the Road 1

2 Coming of Age 16

3 When Life as an Adult Began 36

4 Petoskey and Life after Seminary 54

5 Becoming Hoosiers Again 71

6 Glorious Salad Days on the Prairie 86

7 The Road from Bloomington to Fort Worth
   to Kansas City. 104

8 Marvels and Oddities: Ministry's Sideshow. 123

9 Life as a Seminary President 139

10 Retirement as Visiting the County Fair 156

Preface

This extended autobiographical discourse is my telling of my story. It is how I remember things. There are, of course, shortcomings in relying on one's recollections. Memory does not necessarily possess all the facts or have an unbiased perspective. Consequently, memories will likely produce something that more resembles a water color than a photograph. Roscoe Bell, a friend and mentor, put it more simply. In the Preface to his unpublished autobiography, *Almost Memories,* he wrote, "I think everything in here is true, but I can't be absolutely certain." I begin with that same caveat.

Primarily, this memoir is a gift to my wife, daughters, sons-in-law and grandchildren. Beyond family, I do not anticipate much of an audience. There could be a few people who have known me as a pastor, colleague, friend or acquaintance who will peruse these pages. There might even be a rare descendant who will find the story of a minister in the family in the twentieth and early twenty-first centuries interesting.

That I do not anticipate this volume to be widely read is not disappointing. It is primarily intended as an expression of love for family. Perhaps the most pleasant surprise from this labor has been the personal benefit. It is a very meaningful exercise to put one's life in order and then to reflect on the journey. I heartily recommend memoir writing to others.

My *Sine Qua Non*

From time to time, I will interrupt this narrative to offer a side comment. These will always be in italics and range from important clarifications to funny anecdotes to information insertions. This first aside clarifies the role of my wife in this journey.

Sine Qua Non *is the Latin expression for "without which it could not be." Another translation is "but for." I use the term to refer to my wife, Linda. She is my* Sine Qua Non. *My journey has been dependent on her.*

From time to time in other places, I will make specific comments about our marriage. However, read these pages with the understanding that Linda is my Sine Qua Non. *Whether I happen to mention it or not, but for her, I would not be who I am. She has been integral to my life since we were children. We dated in junior high and early high school. We were close friends throughout secondary school, even when we were not dating. We married a half century ago when we were nineteen and twenty. We were children, young adults, parents and empty nesters together. We thought of ministry as something we did together. In retirement we are discovering how life together just gets better. Robert Browning had it right in RABBI BEN EZRA:*

> Grow old along with me!
> The best is yet to be.
> The last of life,
> for which the first was made;
> Are times in (God's) hand.

As married people we have created a synergy in which each of us is stronger, better, happier, more whole than we could have ever been without each other. As we move beyond the fifty-year marker, there is a sense in which our lives have become so intertwined that it is difficult to imagine one of us without the other. For that reason, the author photograph on the back cover of this book shows both of us. A picture only of me would send an incomplete message about what it took to write this memoir.

Our relationship has made marriage a wondrous thing. I am unable to rationally explain how two people could meet and marry while barely out of childhood, raise children, go through the ups and downs of a half-century together, undergo separate changes and continue to love the person the other has become. I do not know how the miracles of God's grace should be ranked, but this must come close to the top of the list.

The Cueni Family, Summer, 2012

We Make Much but Not All of Our Road by Walking

The Spanish writer Antonio Machado has a line in one his poems, *Se hace camino al andar*. It translates, "You make your road by walking" and asserts that the course of our life is not predetermined. You take charge of your own destiny by assessing options and making choices.

Within significant limits, I agree with Machado. Certainly much of my life has been constructed by my choosing between and among options. Challenges appeared and were either resolved or avoided. Choice led to choice; way turned on to way. At any junction, different, often seemingly insignificant choices could have propelled me onto a very different path. I accept responsibility for the road I traveled. It was made by my walking.

At the same time, I reject the notion that everything was of my choosing. There are serious limits to self-determination.

I had no say in many of life's most determinative factors. I was not given a choice of the genes I inherited, when and where I was born or how I was raised. I may have made my road by walking, but my choices would have been very different if I had been born in a rural village in a developing country or with a serious mental or physical handicap.

I am equally convinced that even though part of my road was made by my choices and part was determined by circumstances beyond my control, God was also in the midst of my life, shaping and directing my course. To illustrate, I believe God called me into ministry. I could have said "No." I was always free to decide a different career path. In retrospect, however, I believe God continued to place options before me that led me through a maze of decisions and opportunities into ministry. I have never been absolutely certain how God was in the midst of this and other decisions. I am simply convinced that God was and is.

This explanation may seem confusing, even contradictory. There is good reason for that. Determining how a life takes a certain course is seldom clear, simple and straightforward. As a small child I lived in public housing. I had no say in that or in many other aspects of my early childhood. On the other hand, at a very early age I made a decision to change the course of my life. That childhood decision was, in retrospect, a remarkable assertion of self-determination. As a young adult I worked as a Venereal Disease Investigator in the urban core of Detroit and later in rural areas of western Michigan. Even though I did this for less than two years, it was an incredibly formative influence in my life.

My experience as a VD investigator moved me into ministry and laid a foundation for a number of my core theological constructs. Somehow a childhood in public housing and an early adult experience in communicable disease investigation resulted in a more than forty-year ministry that included about three and a half decades as pastor of local congregations. I finished my working career as a Seminary President. Certainly this journey would not have been readily predicted from my inauspicious beginning. I have come to account for it, at least in part, as the leading of God.

The end of the poem by Antonio Machado stresses the transitory nature of our journey. To paraphrase the imagery of Machado, "As you turn to look back, you see a path that your feet will never travel again. Then, wayfarer, your road appears as the wake behind a ship."

That is, indeed, true. With what seems unexpected suddenness, I figuratively find myself standing on the deck of a constantly moving ship looking back. Rather than substantial and enduring, the course of my life seems as froth on the water. Even the foamy memory of the journey will be soon lost if not quickly recorded. That realization has moved me to put my recollections on paper.

1

First Steps down the Road

President Franklin D. Roosevelt described Pearl Harbor Day as "December 7, 1941, a day that shall live in infamy." On that day, my mother was well into her pregnancy with me. I don't know exactly what I was doing. Perhaps I was growing ears or marking the significance of Pearl Harbor Day in some other way. The point is that the Second World War was freshly underway by the time I was born. I was to be one of the children of America's Greatest Generation. As every child born in that era, I was nurtured in the soil of stories of how the adults in the neighborhood had endured the Great Depression and saved the world for democracy by their service in the military or on the home front.

On Friday the thirteenth of February 1942, less than three months after the President and Congress declared war on Japan, I was born in Akron, Ohio, at Saint Thomas Hospital to Dawn Hall Cueni and Richard Stinson Cueni. The day I was born, Mom was four months short of her 20th birthday. Dad was a few months short of twenty-four. Both were high school graduates. In fact, they had married on June 15, 1940, the week after Mom graduated. According to the U.S. Census, a few months prior to his marriage, my father was living with his parents working "in sales, delivering brochures door to door." Before or soon after they married, he got a job at Goodyear Tire and Rubber, a position better suited to a family man.

My mother's father was a plumber. Dad's father was a sheet metal worker. My parents could be described as "just folks who came from families of just folks." Although ordinary working people, each of my parents could trace at least some family members back into American history. My mother's family boasted a direct lineage to the early settlers of the Dutch Colony, New Amsterdam, present day New York City. Mom's ten great grandfather, Evardus Bogardus, was the second pastor of Marble Collegiate Church in lower Manhattan. In the book, *The Island in the Center of the World* (Russell Shorto, 2005), Bogardus is described as the short, beer-swilling parson who led the opposition against the Governor of the colony. Evardus died in a ship wreck while returning to the Netherlands on official colony business in 1641.

Another branch of Mom's family is traced to an Irishman named Owen Fee. He emigrated from the northern part of Ireland in the 1840s and worked as a farm hand in western New York. In the fall of 1861, thirty-nine years of age with a pregnant wife and eight children, he volunteered for the Union Army. Owen Fee was killed in the Battle of Fair Oaks, also called Seven Pines, not far from Richmond, Virginia about seven months after he left New York.

I have wrestled with why a man with a wife and soon-to-be-nine children would volunteer for the war and have concluded he was probably seeking a quieter life.

My father's mother, Ruth Stinson Cueni, traced a branch of her family to a Milton Massachusetts man who served in the Revolutionary War. His name was Nathaniel Houghton, and this lineage still serves any family member yearning to join the Sons or Daughters of the American Revolution.

Ruth Cueni's maternal grandfather was a Union soldier and blacksmith named A.H. Cole. He was living near Racine, Wisconsin in the summer of 1861 when he volunteered with the 22nd Wisconsin infantry. This regiment was strongly anti-slavery. It was commanded by a rabid abolitionist who had worked with the Wisconsin Underground Railroad. The regiment has a fascinating story. It involves a law partner of Mary Todd Lincoln's father, hiding escaped slaves in regimental ranks, defying the policy of the Union General commanding forces in Kentucky, the intervention of President Lincoln and a special act of Congress ten years after the end of the Civil War.

Unfortunately, A.H. Cole paid little attention to this grand swirl of history. He deserted the regiment on Christmas Day, 1862. He returned to Wisconsin, moved the family to Ohio, joined two more regiments of the Union Army and served until June, 1865, a few months after the war ended. At his discharge, Grandfather Cole was demoted for conduct unbecoming a soldier. According to the National Archives in Washington, D.C., he had lost part of his tent. Twenty years after the war, he was disabled by a major occupational hazard for a nineteenth century blacksmith, arthritis, and applied for a veteran's pension. The man from the government who made the home visit wrote a letter for his permanent file that said, to paraphrase, "this man strikes me as a lazy good-for-nothing." As a widow, his wife received his Civil War pension.

The Cueni family name does not have a long history in the United States. As close as my research can tell, Frederick Cueni, my great-grandfather came to Independence, Ohio with his mother and two adult brothers about 1870. Frederick worked in a stone quarry in Switzerland and had the same job in this country. He married, adopted the daughter his wife had by a previous relationship and had a few children of his own—including my grandfather, Frank Cueni. Both Frederick and his wife died before their children came of age. As a teenager, my grandfather lived with his eldest sister, the daughter Frederick had adopted.

Our Cueni name is rather rare in the United States, but rather common along the Birs River south of Basel, Switzerland. We have traveled there and about 5-10 percent of the population has the name. I once found a late fourteenth century reference to a man named Cueni paying taxes/tribute to the landowner. Cueni is, obviously, an old name. The family in Switzerland is German speaking. I don't know for sure, but I suspect the name is spelled with a "C" rather than the Germanic "K" because the Birs River Valley is near French-speaking Switzerland.

I must admit that a nearly unpronounceable family name with more vowels than consonants has been a lifelong source of delight. To this day when strangers hesitate or stumble over the pronunciation, I try to set them at ease. "Please call me what my friends call me... SIR!"

All was not ideal with Richard and Dawn Cueni when their baby boy was born. The story of how I came to be called Bob illustrates this. When I was a teenager, my mother told me that while she was pregnant, my father wanted to name me Anselm Stinson Cueni. Mom did not concur. She thought that if I was named Anselm, people would not know how to pronounce either my first or last name.

She went on to say my father was not at the hospital when I was born. A nun came into her room and asked what had been decided for the baby's name. Without waiting to consult with her husband she told the nun, "Name him Richard after his father and Robert because I like the name."

As a boy, I was simply Bob Cueni. My legal and professional name was R. Robert Cueni. Only as I moved into my supernumerary years have I begun to use Richard Robert. Social Security and the need to match my passport and driver's license with the name on an airline ticket have required it.

My Parents' Wedding

When I became a young adult, my mother completed the story of my naming. My father had not simply missed my birth by an hour or two. As was common at that time, Mom was in the hospital for the better part of a week and my Dad did not visit her until I was three days old. As my mother explained, my father was busy with his girlfriend, Leona McNabb. She eventually became his wife and my stepmother.

Although I doubted this part of the story for years, I have learned it is true. Among my stepmother's possessions at her death was the visitor registration book from her father's funeral. While my mother was in the hospital recovering from my birth, Richard Cueni, my father, signed as an attendee of the funeral of William McNabb, Leona's father.

Incidents like this help to explain why I have no memory of my parents being married, why my mother seldom said a nice thing about my father and why I do not remember my parents having an informal face-to-face conversation until I was forty. It was not an amicable parting, particularly from my mother's perspective.

The Reason I Was to be Named ANSELM

In recent years, I have discovered that my father had a logical reason to suggest I be named Anselm. That was his saint's name. He was Richard Stinson Anselm Cueni. Dad was a namesake of Saint Anselm, the brilliant eleventh century monk who developed the Ontological Argument for the Existence of God. Dad wanted to share the name with me. As a child I would have hated being called Anselm, but I would have loved it as an adult.

My parent's divorce was dispatched without delay. By my second birthday, Richard was married to Leona and they had a three-week-old son, my brother David. By my third birthday, Mom and her second husband, Fred Fritz, had a daughter, my sister Donna.

I have memories of living in an apartment in Akron's public housing during Mom's marriage to Fred. I never inquired as to the reasons behind that. We could have been living in public housing because of the post-war housing shortage or because we were on welfare. Certainly financial resources were limited.

Mom did not have a washing machine. She did the laundry in the bathtub on a washboard. Rather than an electric refrigerator, a deliveryman furnished blocks of ice for an icebox.

To a present generation these living conditions may seem unfortunate. It was not experienced that way. Whatever a child is doing at the moment is considered normal. I do not remember feeling underprivileged or deprived of anything particular for having lived in public housing.

On the other hand, I have memories of being terrified of my mother's second husband while living there. I assume it was his drinking that led to frequent angry rants and rages. I remember one particularly terrifying night that Mom, Donna and I fled to a neighbor's apartment while Fred proceeded to scream and throw the furniture around our apartment. I think Fred's behavior did more to influence my childhood than simply living in public housing.

Mom ended her marriage with Fred Fritz because he was verbally and physically abusive. That divorce resulted in Mom, Donna and me moving in with her parents, Floyd and Hazel Hall. Every young boy should live in the same house with loving grandparents, an adoring mother and a beautiful baby sister.

In the early 1940s, Akron was an industrial city of about 200,000–300,000 people. A plethora of international rubber companies produced tires for the Allied war effort. After the war, the city returned to producing truck and automobile tires for the domestic market. During and after the war this boom city welcomed workers from rural Appalachia as well as a host of immigrants, mostly from Eastern and Southern Europe. Akron in the 1940s and 1950s was a vital place of opportunity with significant religious, ethnic and racial diversity.

My grandparents' house was on Betty Street, near a Johnson Street shopping area, in the rubberized shadow of Goodyear Tire and Rubber Company. If the wind blew from one of the rubber plants, the area smelled like smoked ham—after the ham spoiled. My memory is that in the winter, the snow quickly turned black from tiny bits of floating rubber mixing with the snow.

Frank H. Mason Elementary, where I attended, was within walking distance. An old man operated a candy store on the street that led to the school. The neighborhood had plenty of kids my age. Only an occasional passing automobile interrupted our games in the street. A nearby empty wooded lot provided a convenient place to capture garter snakes. The lawn on a warm summer evening glowed with fireflies. The neighborhood movie house had the grand name of the Royal Theater. A child's admission was fourteen cents. Weekend matinees included two feature films, five cartoons, a newsreel, and a twenty-minute serial about a superhero or cowboys and Indians. Nearly every kid in the neighborhood went to the Royal on Saturday afternoon and then again on Sunday afternoon when the feature films changed.

Life was good for a couple of years when things changed again. Mom had been working the evening shift in a factory. One morning at breakfast, she told Grandma Hall, "I met the nicest man at work last night. His name is John Strizak."

When I was about seven years old, Mom and John married. He was her third husband. She had yet to turn twenty-seven. Looking back, I can explain this only by saying that turmoil reigned during and after WWII. Many people, my mother included, made personal decisions on significant issues without all the facts and without considering possible long-term consequences.

When they first married, the four of us, Mom, John, Donna and I, lived in three or four upstairs rooms at Grandma and Grandpa Hall's house. Our rooms had been remodeled as an apartment.

It was not a satisfactory arrangement, particularly after Grandpa Hall's death. Grandma didn't care for John and regularly told him her reasons in a loud, clear voice. Grandma frequently fought with John, but then, so did Mom. As a person, John had some fine qualities. He was a hard worker, a good provider, honest to a fault and faithful to his marital vows. From his ethnic background, John introduced me to Polka music. When the least downhearted, my spirits are still lifted by streaming the website, www.247polkaheaven.com.

I am thankful for John's best qualities. Unfortunately, these were obscured by the fact that he was also proved to be an angry, controlling, verbally abusive, obsessive-compulsive patriarch. Consequently, my mother's initial nice man assessment did not survive the test of time.

For this little boy, Mom's marriage was experienced as moving through an open door into a different world. I went from being my mother's adored child who seldom did anything wrong to being a stepson who was incapable of doing anything right. No matter how hard I tried, I could not please this new man in our lives. My mother had trusted me to walk down the street to play with friends. John did not trust me to stand alone on the front porch. Not that I was singled out. Mom, Donna and I lived under John's controlling dominance. We went from living virtually without stress to lives of unrelenting tension.

Among other difficulties, I came to quickly realize that John lacked basic parenting skills. I vividly remember him teaching me to tie my shoe laces. He placed me on the living room couch and told me to watch. He tied my shoe. "Now you try it," he said.

At that point, my fine motor skills could be made worse only by wearing boxing gloves. I tried to tie my shoe and failed miserably. He whacked me on the head and demonstrated the skill a second time. "Try it again," he said. I did and still failed. This prompted another whack on the head and another demonstration of proper shoe-tying technique. This process was repeated over and over again until I could tie my shoelaces—sort of.

In addition to mastering basic shoelace tying, I received important life lessons. Among these are: (1) If you persevere through stress, pain and the inappropriate behavior of others, you can accomplish what otherwise might be impossible and (2) No matter how you try, some people simply cannot be pleased. These are lessons that have served me well into my adult life.

An Attempt to Explain a Stepfather

In fairness, John's shortcomings need to be assessed in light of his background. I have come to understand that being an angry, controlling, verbally abusive, obsessive-compulsive patriarch was his way to cope with the vagaries of life. He believed that if he could control the people and circumstances in the world around him, he could hold at bay the capricious irregularities of the chaos that was his early life.

His behavior, of course, resulted from the road he traveled. His birth parents, John and Julia Rigan, emigrated in 1913 from

Hungary. John's father, a deep shaft coal miner, and his two-year-old sister died within days of each other during the Spanish Flu Epidemic of 1918. John was only six months old when his mother was widowed. After his father's and sister's deaths, his mother, with little education or English fluency, went to work in a factory as a rubber polisher.

As best I can discern, she married George Strizak about fifteen months after her first husband's death. He was a Slovakian coal miner who had immigrated from near Prague. If my childhood memories are accurate, he was the most likely model for John's becoming an angry, controlling, verbally abusive, obsessive-compulsive patriarch.

Mom and John, 1949, their wedding year.

Family circumstances were hard during John's growing-up years. Even in the economically booming 1920s, his stepfather worked six or seven days each week while his family remained poor. They lived in a company-owned house and shopped at the company-owned store. In the years before the United Mine Workers union found its way into mines worked by George Strizak, his twelve-hour shift frequently ended with bringing the family's dinner, a bucket of soup, home from the company-operated welfare food kitchen. This deeply embarrassed a proud man and his family.

To add another layer of sadness, John's older brother Michael was murdered at the age of sixteen. The only explanation I have heard is that he was killed in a dispute over a moonshine delivery. As if that is not enough, John's first marriage, from which he had two sons, was relationally and financially devastating. Because of the road he traveled, he was very untrusting of others.

For John, education was not a core value. He advocated hard work as the only reliable path to a decent life. Everything indicates his formal education stopped early so that he could pay his own way by working in a coal mine. He once showed me a payday receipt. The date on the pay stub indicated that he was a late adolescent when he received it. He explained that he was paid for the back-breaking work of digging and loading coal at fifty cents per ton.

I do not know how much education John received. He never mentioned going to school. He took the Akron Beacon Journal and perused it daily. He may have read every word. He may have simply looked at the pictures and read the headlines. There were no books or other reading material in the house. He could sign his name, but I never saw him write a personal letter or even a note to himself.

I never heard his mother or stepfather speak more than a few words of heavily accented English. They spoke a foreign language to each other. Since they came from different countries, I cannot say with certainty what that language was. Most people of their generation living in Stewartsville, a tiny southern Ohio coal mining town, did not speak English fluently.

I never heard John speak a single word of any foreign language. Instead, he was fluent in what one might call Basic English. His conversation was usually limited to a few words about the outrageous price of gasoline, the lack of rain for the garden, or the progress on the next United Rubber Workers contract with Goodyear. I never heard him engage in extended discussion of a complex idea. To say more than fifteen consecutive words seemed to require him to be angry. Once in that emotional state, his words flowed.

In 1946, at the age of twenty-eight, near financial ruin and emotionally hurting from a recent divorce, he left the coal fields and moved to Akron in search of opportunity. He found it through self-

reliance and hard work. At his death in September 2001, he left an estate of nearly half a million dollars; not bad for a man who once dug coal for fifty cents per ton.

It also needs to be added that out of the struggle through which he had passed, John became an advocate of social justice, particularly for those he believed were not fairly rewarded for their labor. As a boy, he saw firsthand the difference in living conditions before and after the organization of the United Mine Workers. He had learned from observation that the UMW had in mind the best interest of the miners and their families, not the coal company management. When he came to Akron, he not only joined the United Rubber Workers, he served as an elected union representative for many years. To him, the Union was not simply the way workers sought higher wages; it was the way workers were insured fair treatment and safe working conditions.

In the late 1960s, Caesar Chavez, who was organizing Hispanic farm workers in California, called for a national grape boycott to force vineyard owners into collective bargaining. John, an Ohio rubber worker and son of immigrants, took on the cause of Mexican farm workers in California. He knew from experience that workers needed a voice in the workplace.

At first, there were no grapes purchased in the Strizak house. Then, as some owners began to bargain with the United Farm Workers and others didn't, he took to the time to learn which did and which didn't. He bought only Union-picked grapes. When the boycott was extended to lettuce, he supported that.

His behavior explains why, with a bit of admitted hyperbole, I have frequently noted that "In the Strizak household, 'Union' and 'God' were interchangeable terms." His belief in the Union helps explain why at his retirement, they said of him, "He never missed a union meeting."

John Strizak was the way he was because of the circumstances he encountered and the choices he made in made in how to respond to those circumstances. That same is true, of course, for all of us.

After Grandpa Hall's death, we lived with Grandma for an extended period. I am not sure for how long. For a child, a month can seem a year, and a year a lifetime. While at her house on Betty Street, I started elementary school. I loved it, but apparently I was not very good at it. I was placed in the first grade slow-to-learn Redbird Reading Circle. I understand why. No one encouraged me to read as a small child. There was not even reading material in the house. When I started school, the concept of reading was a mystery. I learned quickly and was upgraded to another reading group. I don't recall the color of the group's bird logo.

At Mason School, I first became aware of what has been a lifelong problem—color discernment. In first grade, in order to pass the color chart exam, the teacher permitted other kids in the class to whisper the color names as I stood at the chart. Linda still has to give me names for colors.

About that same time, I was hit by a car and spent a couple of weeks in Akron's Children's Hospital. The details remain foggy, but I believe I stepped between parked cars into traffic while trying to cross Johnson Street. A car tossed me into the air and I landed in the street. I had a severely broken nose, several cracked ribs, various contusions and a bruise on my hip that looked curiously similar to the toy cap pistol I was wearing. I also acquired a hard-earned lesson on why adults instruct children to look both ways before crossing the street.

After the first few days of discomfort, Children's Hospital became a playground. I shared a room with about a dozen other children. Once ambulatory, I spent the day making friends with aides, nurses and the other kids. We talked, played games and generally had a great time. More than sixty years later, I remain amazed that I suffer no lingering physical ailment from that accident.

In addition to school and street-crossing etiquette, I was introduced to the church and the Christian faith while living on Betty Street. The pastor of Williard Evangelical and Reformed Church at the corner of Betty and Johnson Streets was a fellow of German heritage named Schmuck. He had ascended to this less-than-prestigious pulpit after his father completed a few decades as minister. I began attending Sunday School at Williard E & R and absolutely loved it. I have no memory of what precipitated my attendance. Mom or a neighbor may have taken me. I do clearly remember that the people of that faith community welcomed this little boy.

I still recall a Sunday School lesson on the Parable of the Good Samaritan. We acted out the story again and again until every member of the class had an opportunity to play every role—including the donkey that carried the beaten man to the inn. That remains my favorite parable. In fact, the message of the Parable of the Good Samaritan forms a central theological construct of my understanding of the Gospel. To paraphrase briefly a sermon I have preached many times: *A man was traveling from the orderliness of Jerusalem to Jericho, a city at the edge of the wilderness. Thieves beat, robbed and left the man seriously injured at the side of the road. After religious leaders passed him by, an outsider, a Samaritan stopped to help.*

In like manner, we live our lives traveling that short road between Jerusalem and Jericho, that is, between order and chaos. At the most unexpected moment, serious difficulty can descend, overwhelm order and replace it with chaos. When we are beaten and suffering at the edge of the road, we need someone to stop and help.

Mom and I

As a child, I experienced Betty Street from the Williard E & R Church to our house as a Jericho Road. In one block I often went from acceptance, peace and order at the church to a tension-filled home where I did not know what was going to happen next. My Good Samaritan was the Williard E & R faith community. Because of this, I have often had to admit that I have thought of myself as saved by the Church before I understood the meaning of salvation in Christ.

With some regularity during those years, we visited John's family in southeastern Ohio. John had come of age up not far from the Ohio River, about a dozen miles from Wheeling, West Virginia. Stewartsville was a tiny town of perhaps 100 houses, a tavern or two, and all that remained of the coal mine that once attracted workers to the area.

The Strizak house was a less-than-modest clapboard dwelling on the side of a well-worn Appalachian mountain. The house had electricity but no indoor plumbing. Personal business was accomplished in an immaculate backyard outhouse. When John was a child, a spring supplied the family's water through a gravity-fed pipe into a side yard wooden trough. When I was a child that was still the family's water source for baths and irrigating the garden. John's mother continued to use rainwater for the laundry. This was collected in barrels kept beneath house downspouts. The drinking water came from a hand pump that had been installed on a kitchen counter.

The dominant geological feature of Stewartsville was an enormous hill of coal-mining waste directly across from the house. That pile must have been 75–100 feet tall with a diameter of 200–300 feet. When the mine was still working, stony material had been loosened from inside the mountain by miners trying to get to the vein of coal. The resulting slag heap was composed of tiny bits of coal, black stone that was not quite coal and other assorted rock. Chemical waste from mining turned area streams various shades of orange. Vegetation was scarce. The scene was of environmental devastation—polluted water, heavy stench of sulfur, a chemically scorched earth dominated by that small mountain of ugliness.

In other words, it was a place of unlimited adventure for a little boy. I loved to scramble up Slagheap Mountain to throw stones toward the bottom. Hours of delight came by climbing on whatever remained of mining equipment and leftover wooden support structures. The biggest thrill, however, came by wading in the streams to collect the crayfish and frogs that somehow managed to survive the pollutants.

Trips to Stewartville, Ohio, taught great lessons in the importance of looking for opportunities for life and its available joy in the midst of otherwise difficult circumstances.

2

Coming of Age

"When I was ten years of age, I decided to leave Akron and move to Munroe Falls to live with my father and his family."

I have made this statement for the past sixty years. As a septuagenarian, it seems preposterous that a ten-year-old could or would make a decision of such magnitude. It is, however, an essentially true memory. At ten I decided to change my residence.

My desire to move had nothing to do with my mother or her treatment of me. I could not have had a more encouraging, supportive parent. To her dying day, she was my greatest advocate. The issue was my stepfather. As I grew, I became more independent. John's desire to control grew as I matured. When I wanted to play with neighborhood kids, he wanted me to stay in the house where he could keep an eye on me. When I wanted to remain after school to help the teacher clean the blackboard, he demanded that I walk into the house no later than fifteen minutes after school dismissed. Conflict escalated until from my perspective things became intolerable.

Déjà Vu All Over Again
This pattern repeated throughout his life. John was always lov-ing and tolerant with infants and toddlers. As soon as a child be-gan to defy his absolute control, his relationship with and attitude

toward that child began to deteriorate. This is well illustrated by his relationship with Angie, my sister's eldest and his first grandchild. When she was born, there was not a better treated child on the planet. He lavished her with attention, praise and gifts. Eventually, Angie became a normal teenager—as independent as a hog on ice. Consequently she was a constant source of irritation and disappointment to her grandfather.

I have often wondered what would have happened to their relationship if Angie had remained compliant and totally obedient. Other than stifling her emotional development, I have concluded that not much would have been different. After all, no one could ever really please this man or live up to his expectations.

Eventually John learned to deal with his control issues by transferring his affection to small dogs, particularly Yorkshire terriers. A Yorkie never grows much larger than a newborn; will usually stay within sight of the owner; maintains the dreaming innocence and enthusiasm of a child; can, with effort, be trained to sit in the owner's lap for hours on end; and in exchange for lifelong loyalty, expects only a chew toy and a continual supply of doggy snacks.

After what was to me an indeterminate time in Grandma's upstairs apartment, Mom and John purchased a house on McGowan Street, about ten blocks from Betty Street. The house cost $4,500 and had a living room, dining room and kitchen on the first floor with two bedrooms and a bath on the second. The basement, typical of the era, had a furnace, coal storage area and sneeze-inducing mustiness. We had plumbing and electricity, but no telephone. The family at the end of the block had the only phone on the street. If there was an emergency call, it was delivered to the appropriate home by the eldest son of the family with the phone.

The neighborhood was a step down economically from where we lived with Grandma. In addition to rubber factory laborers, some on Betty Street were supervisors, skilled workers and entry-level management. On McGowan Street everyone was blue collar labor. The McGowan Street folks frequently were not employed at a tire factory. Consequently fewer were members of a trade union, and the income on McGowan Street was lower than on Betty Street.

The McGowan community was also not the social equivalent of Betty Street. A son of the neighbors to the left eventually went to prison. To the right of our house was an unpaved alley. One of my playmates lived in a small house at the end of that narrow passageway. His family immigrated, I believe, from Hungary. He once told me that his favorite meal was chicken feet soup. Even as a small boy, I realized that in America not many ranked this a favorite meal. The neighbors across the street threw their empty tin cans and garbage off the back porch onto a continually growing pile of trash. Although I don't think it had anything to do with the open garbage heap they kept, one of their children died of spinal meningitis. Life on McGowan Street in the late 1940s and early '50s did not resemble the middle class of the movies and early television. In fact, it may not have matched the socio-economics of public housing.

I had lobbied my mother for a parent custody change from the time we moved to McGowan Street. She always countered my argument by telling me I could not make that decision until I was ten. When I turned ten, I made the case again with my mother. With a tentative positive answer, I apprehensively sought John's permission.

The obvious question is "How does a 10-year-old boy negotiate a parental custody change?" The obvious answer, of course, is that he doesn't. My mother had to relinquish custody. My father had to accept custody. The court had to agree. Those were issues for adults, not a little boy.

Mom frequently shared that it was the most painful decision she ever made. She did it, however, because she believed it was in my long-term best interest. Her marriage to John was not healthy, but it was her third marriage. There was no reason to assume another divorce and remarriage would improve things. John had adopted Donna. Mom decided to make the best of her present relationship. She also realized her son was not going to flourish living in the same house. "Bobby," as she always called me, "needed an opportunity so I gave up custody." Although he never said, my leaving must have been a relief for John. I cannot imagine he enjoyed trying to train this independent-minded son of his wife.

I am unaware of the Cueni family thought process. Neither Leona nor my father ever discussed it with me. They must, however, have known or at least suspected how discombobulating this custody change was going to be. They had two small sons, David and Jon, eight and seven years of age. Their family structure and routine were established. Bringing a ten- year-old boy into their home was going to significantly rearrange family dynamics. Dad had left his job at Goodyear Tire and Rubber a few years previously and had started what was by that time a growing construction business, primarily building free-standing garages. He worked long hours at the office during the day and many evenings made sales calls somewhere in the metropolitan area. Frequently, other than to sleep at night, he was home only at the dinner hour. Consequently, most parental duties fell to Leona.

Perhaps they decided to accept custody because they too believed it would be in my best long-term interest. Perhaps they thought they owed it to me because of their relationship prior to my birth. Whatever the reasons for accepting custody, if they did not have reservations, they should have.

My primary contribution to the custody decision was lobbying for a change. Reports from the extended family are that I was a precocious child who possessed a great deal of *chutzpah*. I am sure I also had an audacious sense of entitlement. After my positive experience living with Mom and the Halls before the marriage to John, I knew there was a better way to live, and I was sufficiently self-confident to think I deserved that better life.

When permission was granted for me to move to Munroe Falls, I was thrilled. On the other hand, thoughts of the pain my mother experienced in giving custody of her only son to her ex-husband's care still haunt me. In recent years, Donna has shared with me her sense of abandonment when I left the Strizak household. I deeply regret the pain I caused them, but do not regret pushing for the change. I confess, however, that I had my own best interest in mind, not the best interest of either my mother or sister. In the Bible, the highest standard of behavior toward others is to lay down one's life for a friend. I settled for the commercial airline standard to put your own oxygen mask on first before trying to help anyone else.

Whereas one might excuse my behavior on the fact I was only a child, it is not the only time I have had to admit I failed to live up to the highest standards of the faith I claim.

Dad and Leona's wedding

Life at Cuenis

The move to Munroe Falls was everything I had hoped it would be. The Cueni family was affirming and welcoming. Dad and Leona went out of their way to include me and make me feel like one of the family. I loved the school and meeting new friends. Even making visits to Strizaks went better than living there. I felt considerably less stressed as a weekend guest than as a resident.

The Cuenis had plans to vacation on Lake Erie the summer I joined the family. A somewhat rustic cottage was rented in a cluster of other rustic cottages near Huron, Ohio. David, Jon, Leona and I spent four blissful weeks on a bluff overlooking Lake Erie. Dad continued to run his business during the week and came on weekends.

For three young boys it was a memorable month. We learned to swim and spent hours practicing that new skill. We fought mythic sea battles while floating atop inflated truck tubes. When the weather was not conducive to swimming, we sharpened our shuffle board skills.

The year after that glorious month on Lake Erie things underwent a dramatic change. Leona fell ill with a recurrence of rheumatic fever. She had bouts of this malady as a child, but this incident was much more severe. Bed rest was the standard treatment of the time. Leona spent well over a year in bed and then several months in a wheelchair before she was sufficiently strong to resume her household, parental and business duties.

Other complications ensued. In hopes of speeding recovery, her physician began to treat her with massive doses of cortisone, the miracle drug of the early 1950s. At that time, the side effects from overuse were not fully understood. Within a few years she developed serious diabetes and rheumatoid arthritis. Family lore held that these diseases were caused by the rheumatic fever and/or the cortisone treatments. Whether that is true or not, I do not know.

In addition, early in Leona's illness, Dad injured his back lifting her from one bed to another. That led to surgery for a ruptured disc. Back surgery would not become common practice for another decade or more. Rather than physical therapy, the rehabilitation protocol of the era called for extended bed rest under the supervision of a physician. Consequently, Dad was in an Akron hospital for more than three months.

With Leona in a hospital bed in an upstairs bedroom and Dad in the hospital, Grandma Hazlet, Leona's mother, moved into the house to care for her bedridden daughter and three boys, ages 8, 9 and 11. My wife tells me she first heard about me during the illnesses of Dad and Leona. Linda's mother often came home from Women's Circle meetings at First Christian Church with tales of how the parents of the three little Cueni boys were too sick to care for them and the church members were taking meals to the house.

For Richard and Leona this had to have been an incredibly difficult time. Dad did not work for nearly half of the year. Leona was out of commission for much longer. Without the presence of either in the day-to-day operations of Cueni Construction Company, business must have been terrible. Family finances must have been a nightmare. The verbal as well as physical communication between them was limited by incapacitating illness. Their marriage had to have been stressed. Each must have dealt with considerable personal pain and physical weakness. Struggle and worry must have been considerable.

Yet, David, Jon and I remember this as a time we simply went about the task of being kids. We felt and acted as though having incapacitated parents was normal. We were basically oblivious to any consequences of their illnesses. Children are amazingly adaptive, resilient creatures.

Eventually things around the Cueni household resumed a more normal pattern. Dad's business expanded to a new location. He added a small lumberyard to his niche of building free-standing garages. After having handled the accounting from home for several years, Leona went to work full time at the new location as the office manager.

Whether or not it had anything to do with extended illnesses I cannot say. However, in the next couple of years the behavior of each as well as their relationship underwent significant, negative change.

Learning the Value of a Day's Work

For several years after relocating to Cuenis, I continued to return to Strizaks for summer visits of three or more weeks. John's sons, Donny and Johnny, would visit at the same time. John, who provided daily child care while Mom worked, apparently subscribed to the maxim that "idle hands are the devil's playground" because he put us all to work. At first he began a daily purchase of 200–300 pounds of potatoes from nearby farms. We transferred the potatoes to peck baskets and sold them door to door for sixty cents each.

Eventually, we switched to selling blackberries. Unlike potatoes, which had to be first purchased, blackberries were free. Early every morning we loaded into the car, drove to different areas of greater Akron and spent about three hours scrounging through wild blackberry patches. Although we picked as many as fifty-two quarts, we averaged about 25 quarts per day. We sold the berries door to door in the afternoon for fifty cents per quart. Sales usually took another two to three hours daily.

Each afternoon, prior to picking up Mom from the plastics manufacturing factory where she worked in production, we were paid for our labor on the basis of what John felt we had earned. We might get as little as thirty-five cents or, on rare occasions, as much as $1–2. Donna received the least because she picked but did not sell berries. Johnny received more than Donny or I because he picked and sold more. My stepfather kept most of the money, in part because he picked more berries than the rest of us combined. He also supplied the transportation as well as room and board. Berry sales were a major source of family income. The United Rubber Workers' union was often on strike during the summer, and the money helped to meet expenses in a cash-strapped household.

In retrospect this was a beneficial way to visit Strizaks. The hours may have been long and the mosquito-infested berry patch unpleasant, but John was much easier to be around when everyone worked. Only when it rained and we could not get into the berry patch was our togetherness stressed. I must also admit I had more spending money than the average kid.

When I was a teenager, I also began to work at the Cueni Construction Company's lumberyard. I helped to load and unload trucks. Before long, I was promoted to the boy in charge of cleaning the saw dust bin and picking up lumber scraps from the warehouse floor. I was first paid $10 for a five-and-a-half day week. On the one hand, that was a large sum of money for a kid my age. On the other hand, it was less than a quarter per hour. If I missed a few hours, the office manager, my stepmother, docked my pay accordingly.

My responsibilities at the lumberyard grew over time. When I acquired a driver's license, I became a truck driver.

By the time I was a high school senior, I was working as a carpenter. Although I was not a very skilled craftsman, the work helped build self-reliance and self-confidence.

When I was ready to take my work experience outside the family, I applied for a job at the town's new Kroger store. On the application I noted that even though I was only sixteen, I had been paid for my work for nearly six years. I got the job. At first, I sacked groceries on weekends. I then trained to run a cash register. Eventually I considered myself the fastest register operator in the store. (Note: the fastest, not the most accurate.) By the end of my time at Kroger, I was the clerk responsible for the toilet paper aisle and the frozen food cases as well as a member of the once-per-week floor scrubbing team. I worked on and off in the grocery store for six years before leaving as a married college graduate. Partly as a result of being a member of the Retail Clerks Union and having a right to collective bargaining, my starting hourly rate of $1.26 eventually advanced to $2.60 plus health and vacation benefits. I actually had to take a $4 per week pay cut to accept the first job that required a college degree.

In my late teens, I worked summers both at Cueni Construction and at Kroger. This was accomplished by working from 8:00–5:00 at the lumber yard and then from 6:00–10:00 at the grocery store. What a blessing. I never had to complain about having nothing to do.

The potato, blackberry, grocery store and lumberyard experiences taught me about the value of hard work. Those lessons served me well throughout my adult life. The evidence demonstrates that I passed the lessons on to my children.

School Teaches More than the 3 Rs

I arrived at Cuenis during the last months of fourth grade and remained in the Stow School system until high school graduation in 1960. I greatly enjoyed the overall school experience, but must admit the academic side of the endeavor held little interest. Learning seemed little more than the price one had to pay for spending the entire day away from home, socializing with friends and playing sports.

That is not to say academic pursuits were neglected. I did what had to be done for grades of A or B with a rare C. That really didn't take much effort. Although I often copied homework from others, I did my own when absolutely necessary. A far better-than-average memory and paying attention to class lectures usually proved sufficient for a respectable grade.

If a subject demanded more, other arrangements were made. For instance, a C in first-year Latin led to not signing up for second-year Latin. Physics and senior mathematics were also avoided because they required understanding the subject matter and not just memorizing it.

This is not to suggest my growing up years were devoid of intellectual curiosity or critical reflection. In sixth grade an interest in geography turned me to regular reading in a set of encyclopedias shelved at the back of the classroom. I also had an early interest in history that was catalyzed by reading *Captain Horatio Hornblower* novels about the British Navy during the Napoleonic War. Probably the most important book of my childhood was John Steinbeck's *The Grapes of Wrath*. I read that book during a stay-at-home illness in eighth grade. It quickened my social conscience about the plight of the poor. Hornblower and Steinbeck motivated me to be a regular reader, if not a serious student. Serious study did not begin until college.

Plenty of Memory on the Hard Drive

My first recollection of how well I could remember comes from second grade. The teacher held up a model of the solar system. She explained the behavior of the planets, their relationship to the sun as well as the difference between the earth rotating on its axis and its revolving around the sun. After giving her little speech once, she put the model on her desk and said, "Children we will talk about this again another time." The next week, she picked up the model and said, "Now, does anyone remember anything about this?"

I raised my hand and repeated everything she had said the previous week. It was probably not word for word, but sufficiently paraphrased. I worried her surprise might cause her to collapse on the classroom floor. She did not realize that I did not understand how the solar system worked. I only remembered and repeated what she said.

This gift of memory has served me well. I can still tell jokes that I heard in grade school. Every Sunday for over three decades, a two thousand word/twenty-minute sermon was written, memorized and delivered without manuscript or note card. At one time, I could challenge people to name a decade between 800 BCE and the present and I would describe something that what was happening. The gift of memory made me a terrific teammate when the game Trivial Pursuit was fashionable.

My wife has correctly observed that my memory is quite selective. She says, "Bob, you remember the infield players on the 1954 Cleveland Indians and interesting facts about daily life in the High Middle Ages, but you cannot remember to take the trash out on Sunday night."

In addition to disposing of household waste, I have never been able to remember people's last names or to memorize poetry. I think the problem with poetry is that it requires word for word recitation and my memory paraphrases. I remain baffled by my problem with people's names. I still remember the Latin names of at least 100 families of insects and trees. I learned those names in undergraduate school in the early 1960s, yet cannot remember the names of human beings I met last month. Memory is a mysterious gift.

On occasion someone will comment on my ability to cite some obscure fact, "Bob, you are so intelligent." I quickly correct them, "No, I have a good memory. There is only a passing correlation between memory and intelligence. I remember many things that I do not comprehend." The movie actor Dustin Hoffman played an autistic savant with profound gifts of observation and memory who could not care for his simplest needs. Hoffman's character was an extreme example of how memory is in a category all its own.

I was in fifth grade when I realized others looked to me for leadership. It was the dead of winter. The usual playground snowball fight was underway during lunch recess. There must have been more than fifty boys participating. About half the participants were hiding in the royal castle, also known as a snow bank. The others were trying to dislodge that group by charging and throwing snowballs. Each time the attackers were repelled.

I arrived late to the fight with a few friends. We joined the attackers. After a few minutes of fierce hand-to-hand combat;

more accurately, a few minutes of lobbing snowballs over the snow bank, I realized that the attacking warriors were looking to me for leadership.

An ingenious master plan began to take shape in my mind. I shouted orders to the boys on the right to outflank those sniveling cowards in the castle. When they were behind the enemy, I was to signal for an attack from the rear. As that group began to prepare the trap I had conceived, I ordered the rest of the boys to lay down a blanket of snowball cover for the flanking maneuver. The plan worked. We drove them out and assumed control of the castle. For the rest of the winter, I assumed daily command of one side or the other in the lunchtime snowball fight.

This was the first experience of others actually valuing what I thought and responding affirmatively to what I suggested. My role as a school leader continued. Three out of four years in high school, I was elected to the Student Council—including Student Counsel Secretary as a sophomore and President as a senior. During my junior year I was not on Student Counsel because I was the Junior Class President. In my graduation year's school annual I am identified as the Leading Man. What that means and how I got that designation remain mysteries even after more than a half-century. It must, however, say something about others recognizing incipient leadership qualities.

Exactly what others saw as leadership ability when I was eleven or twelve or even sixteen or seventeen also remains a mystery. Perhaps there is a leadership pheromone emitted by incipient leaders. On the other hand, maybe others didn't sense any leadership ability at all. Perhaps I simply started to act like a leader; others began to follow and a behavior pattern was established. However they came to be, leadership opportunities in school provided good training in learning how to plan, build a leadership team, motivate constituents and get things done.

In Fairness, a Few Caveats
It needs to be said that whatever identified me as a leader did not carry over into categories of really popular or strikingly handsome. I was never voted Homecoming or Prom King. I did not receive the Best Looking in the Class award. Of course, the academic accolades always went to others.

Some personal recognition must have emanated from an inherent ability to influence faculty, administration and other adults by, shall we say, "kissing up." My father was a charming, even beguiling man. Even though not used for some of his purposes, that gene must have been shared with me.

I also found time for causing trouble. In our senior year, Don Gray and I were president and vice-president of the Student Council. We decided the Stow High building was not only old and poorly maintained, it was downright dirty and even unsafe. With a couple of other senior class leaders we gathered photographs of holes in fire hoses, crumbling steps in the gymnasium balcony, extensive dry rot in the auditorium curtains and dirty floors throughout the building. Our intent was to give a report to the school board and ask that the problems be corrected. Before we could do that the local weekly newspaper caught wind of what we were doing and published an article entitled, "What's Going on Here?" Because nearly every household in the community received this newspaper, our private campaign became very public.

We requested a spot on the agenda of the next meeting of the school board. When our time came, the newspaper reporter was, as usual, present. The board members listened carefully to our presentation, thanked us for taking our student leadership positions seriously and told us they would take the matter under consideration. A few days later we learned of their response. In executive session, they passed a resolution saying student leaders were no longer permitted to appear before the school board. The powers that be had judged that our good intentions had drifted into causing trouble.

At the very end of that school year the same senior class leaders crossed the line from causing trouble to being in trouble. At the Honor's Day Assembly, five or six of us received nearly every top honor for leadership, citizenship, academics and athletics. At the close of the assembly we decided that we did not want to go back to class. We asked Rich Myers's mother to write each of us an excuse so that we could go swimming for the rest of the day.

These notes were not intended to deceive. They were identically worded on identical pieces of paper with obviously forged parental approvals. As I recall, my note said, "Please excuse Bob Cueni from school today. He wants to go swimming. Thank you, Mrs. Cueni." We assumed the good-natured whimsy of our actions would be self-evident.

We returned to school the next day to learn that many on the faculty were not amused. Instead of enjoying our prank, our actions precipitated an emergency faculty meeting. We were told the meeting began with a heated debate on whether our group should be simply killed or killed and eaten. This was followed by serious consideration of expelling us for the rest of the school year and making us repeat our senior years. In the end, the faculty agreed to sentence us to after-school detention and a sit-down meeting with Principal Bill Barr.

Fortunately, Mr. Barr did not agree with those faculty members who fretted that bad behavior on the part of leading students signaled the fall of Western civilization. He pretended to be angry, but the smirk that kept creeping into the corner of his lips gave him away. We dutifully served after-school detention. The incident remains one of my favorite school memories.

Participating in sports was an integral part of growing up. Little League baseball began during fourth or fifth grade. Because I am left handed, I was assigned to play first base. Frankly, I was never particularly skilled in the field. At the plate, I was somewhat better. In fact, I learned the mechanics of hitting well enough to hit the ball a significant distance with some regularity. I played organized baseball until I the spring of my junior year when I began working at Kroger.

Football was a regular fall activity from seventh through twelfth grades. When I began playing at age twelve and 5'4", I was one of the bigger kids. My father was 6'2" and well over two hundred pounds. The coach must have thought I would grow to Dad's size. Consequently, he assigned me to play on the offensive line—where size is critical. Unfortunately, I only grew one more inch and never weighed more than 140 pounds. Because I was also slow and not particularly gifted at catching, kicking or throwing the ball, I kept playing the guard position. Opposing defensive linemen frequently outweighed me by 50 to 100 pounds.

In spite of a height, weight and skill level disadvantage, I played in nearly every game each year of high school. Rather than ability, this can be attributed to how poorly our team performed. The Stow Bulldogs were terrible. In four years, our wins did not total more than a half dozen. Jim Tyree, our coach, was quoted in the Akron Beacon Journal, "Being the coach at Stow has made me a more patient Christian."

As might be imagined, I have never longed to relive my football glory years. Instead I have come to understand that learning to get over a loss teaches a more valuable lesson than always winning.

Mr. Tyree was far more successful as wrestling coach. He started the wrestling program during my freshman year. I wrestled all four years at 127 pounds. My sophomore year, I finished fourth in the region. As a junior I finished second in the region and went to the state finals at Ohio State University. During my senior year I was entertaining the possibility of wrestling in college when I separated a shoulder in a Christmas vacation tournament at Hiram College. That ended my wrestling career.

Both wrestling and Jim Tyree were very important. Wrestling was a great builder of self-confidence and taught me lessons on the need to persevere in order to succeed. Coach Tyree both offered encouragement and a positive male role model as I was moving toward manhood.

Life at Cuenis Continued

After the extended illnesses of Dad and Leona, the Cueni household settled into a routine, but it never fully recovered. Finances were never as good. Their marriage was not the same. They were not the same. And, of course, David, Jon and I were not the same.

Many factors contributed. The post-war economic boom slowed and the nation entered a recession. Dad often had to close the business for weeks at a time because of the lack of sales. Dad and Leona frequently disagreed over money. There were also episodes of intense arguing that as an adult I have come to realize were over Dad's relationships with other women. I was into adolescent striving for independence and questioning authority. David and Jon were growing up and showing signs of their impending adolescence. It was a home where relationships were deteriorating, conflict was escalating and there was not a reliable action plan for ameliorating the resulting unhappiness.

These worsening conditions were exacerbated when Dad began to take too many tranquilizers to reduce his anxiety and too many prescription pain pills for his back. To deal with these conditions, on a number of occasions, his doctor admitted him to the hospital psychiatric unit.

As if these were not sufficiently problematic, when I was in junior high, he began to drink heavily. By the time I was a high school junior he was drinking a fifth of distilled alcohol nearly every day. His pattern was to start at the office in the late afternoon and continue drinking until bedtime. Frequently, I came home to find him passed out in the living room. I would help him up the stairs and get him in bed. In order not to have to suffer through a loud disagreement between them, I tried not to wake Leona.

Dad was never the easiest person with whom to live. Even sober he could be cranky and unreasonable. When drunk he was worse. Although never physically abusive, he was sufficiently nasty that I found it best to try to minimize dealing with him.

With Dad out of commission for much of each day, the responsibilities of family and business fell to Leona. She did the job, but it was not easy. It took a toll on her.

Partly due to these changes in the family dynamics and partly due to the normal stressful adolescent passage, my last few years in the Cueni house were not particularly pleasant. There were frequent conflicts with Dad and/or Leona. Consequently, I tried to be at home as little as possible. When not working or participating in sports, I kept busy with friends, school and church youth group activities.

The Growing Importance of the Church

I was a regular at Sunday School while I lived at Strizaks. When I moved to Cuenis, Leona was insistent on Sunday School and Worship attendance. David and Jon were never particularly amenable to the practice, but I loved it. I still have fond memories of Sunday School classes taught by caring, well-intentioned church members. Although Ted Cord's sermons were replete with words beyond my understanding and lasted a very long forty minutes, I not only learned to listen, but think I might have even gained some understanding of the faith from his preaching.

When I was eleven or twelve, a woman in the congregation began to talk with me about making a Confession of Faith and being baptized. I had, of course, been baptized in the Roman Catholic Church shortly after my birth, but in that era at First Christian Church, that didn't count. Rev. Cord, a former Roman Catholic, frequently made a point about baptism being valid only when it is done by immersion when one is old enough to understand its meaning. What did I know? I was a still a kid. I decided for the Confession/Immersion route.

The conversations with that dear woman went on for several weeks before I walked down the aisle during the singing of the last hymn at the close of Sunday worship. I put my hand in the hand of the minister and made my Confession of Faith, "Yes, I believe that Jesus is the Christ, the son of the living God and I accept him as my Lord and Savior." The next Sunday morning, I went into the waters of baptism and was immersed *In the name of the Father, the Son and the Holy Spirit.* It really was one of those Sacred God Moments of life. I remember it very well.

The church continued to grow in importance as I moved into my teen years. In fact, I felt more at home in the church than with the rest of the Cueni family. This was confirmed when my brother David acquired the family home movies taken during that era and made copies. The films show that in my teen years I behaved as though I did not belong. I do not seem to join in the conversations. When others are enjoying themselves, I seldom participate. I stand off to the side and watch. When the family takes a walk in the woods, I am either behind or ahead of the others, never really with them. In those years, I seem to be the answer to the question, "In this scene, who is the guest at the family reunion?"

I don't think others intentionally sent a message of my not belonging. Certainly, no one ever said that in so many words. I own this as my feeling. Other than my imagination, a number of things could have contributed. Physically, I was short and everyone else was tall. David and Jon were blonds. I was a brunette. The rest of the Cueni family stayed together all the time. I left periodically to be with Strizaks.

At the church, on the other hand, I felt as though I belonged. I resonated with the words of Alexander Campbell, one of the nineteenth century founders of the Christian Church (Disciples of Christ): *"You, my friend, once an alien, are now a citizen of heaven: once a stranger, are now brought home to the family of God. You have owned my Lord as your Lord, my people as your people."*

My Life's Partner

Linda Enters the Story

I first knew of Linda Andresen when I was in the sixth grade. Lynn Francis, a fellow member of Mrs. Denny's class, lived close to her and they knew each other. Lynn told me about Linda, whom he described as his girlfriend. He regaled me with stories of their mutual love and described their relationship as one to rival the great romances of history and literature.

Linda has a different memory. She says they walked to school together during their early elementary school years. She describes Lynn as irritating, not loving. He used to hit her with his trombone case as they walked. Of course, Linda did not realize that trombone thumping is universally recognized as way for a young boy to demonstrate affection to a young girl.

When Lynn described the youngest Andresen sister, I realized I knew her from church. As I got to know more about her, I came to understand the accuracy of Lynn Francis's description. Linda Andresen was a young woman of a thousand gifts and charms.

By the time I was in eighth grade and she was in seventh, we were an item at school and church. On Sunday morning we would sit together in the balcony, hold hands as surreptitiously as possible and count the pages on Rev. Cord's sermon manuscript as he turned them. Elizabeth Barrett and Robert Browning could not top that for romantic interlude.

As a freshman, I bought Linda a carnation wrist corsage, took her to the high school homecoming dance and walked her home. We kissed at her back door—the first for each of us. We still, from time to time, mention the thrill of that night. When our junior and early senior high romance ran its course, we remained good friends and regularly spent time together—just talking.

In the fall of my senior year, we both attended an after-school meeting. I had driven and offered her a ride home. When we arrived at her house we remained in the car and talked for an hour or more. It was one of the most formative conversations of my life.

Graduation was in eight months and I didn't have a plan for my future. There had been no chats with either my mother or father about vocational decisions. There was no pressure to work for Cueni Construction Company, although that was a possibility. I assumed I would go on to college, but did not know what that might entail. No one in our family had ever gone beyond high school. Jim Tyree, the football and wrestling coach, was my most positive male role model. I considered becoming a teacher, like Coach Tyree.

In the course of our conversation, Linda said to me: "Bob, I think you should become a minister. You would make a great minister."

A seed was planted and it began to grow. Within a few months, I went to Bethany College and began to prepare to preach the Gospel.

3

When Life as an Adult Began

I chose to go to Bethany College because Marc Arnold, a friend from church, suggested it. Bethany had been founded in 1840 by Alexander Campbell as a school for the training of church leaders in what was to become the Christian Church (Disciples of Christ). I wanted to be a minister in that church. It seemed the place to go.

The total annual cost for tuition, room and board was $1200. By today's standard, that is a pittance, but other Midwest liberal arts schools had similar costs. As a pre-ministerial student I received a scholarship of $500. The remainder was covered by savings I had accumulated over the previous few years. Leona provided $10 per week for incidental expenses.

With three pairs of new pants, five shirts and box of socks and underwear, I headed to Bethany, West Virginia. There were only two-lane roads. The hundred mile trip took more than three hours. I had not visited the college or town before freshman orientation. I was surprised by the beauty of the campus, the size of the village and the isolation of both. Bethany College was far lovelier than the brochure pictures. The town had no more than a few hundred people. The downtown consisted of an old-fashioned General Store, a barber shop, a post office and the local Disciple church. Both town and college were twelve to fifteen miles up and down twisting roads from the nearest anything.

Some found Bethany's size and location problematic. I didn't. The freshman year at Bethany was the best of my growing-up years. I almost never missed a class. I did the assignments. I studied late into the night and again early in the morning. I pledged a fraternity and made new friends. It was wonderful.

The Valuing of Education

As mentioned, no one in Mom's, Dad's, Leona's or John's family ever attended college. For that matter, no family member claimed to have missed anything by not attending college. Higher education was not an expectation, a practice or a value.

For some reason I differed from other members of the family in that I valued education. In fact, in early adolescence, as most boys my age, I contemplated running away from home. Unlike the average kid, I planned to take the two-volume Lincoln Encyclopedia with me so that I could continue my college preparation while on the road.

By the close of my freshman year I had exhausted my savings. Additional funding would be needed to continue at Bethany. I planned to work both at Cueni Construction and Kroger during the summer. In addition, I applied at the college to work in food service my sophomore year. I calculated I was still going to need an additional few hundred dollars. I wrote my Dad to ask for monetary assistance.

He gave me his answer a few days after I arrived home. One evening I went with him on a sales appointment and on the way home we stopped at the Silver Lake Country Club. We went into the bar and he bought me a Rob Roy, i.e., a Scotch Manhattan—pretty big stuff since I was still two years short of the legal age for adult beverages. He proceeded to tell me that he had recently joined that Country Club. It had cost him $2,000. Therefore, he was not able to help me with going back to Bethany. If I wanted to go to college, he told me I could live at home and go to nearby Kent State University. He had learned Kent charged less than $500 per year for tuition, books and fees. He had no plans to give me money nor would he cosign a loan, but I should be able to earn enough for tuition and books. He would supply room and board.

Thus ended my study at Bethany College and, for the time being, my plans to be a minister. By the end of the summer, I was mentally prepared to transfer to Kent State University. My major was changed from Religious Studies to Biology and my career plans shifted from pastoral ministry to high school biology teacher. I had some faint hope of getting back to ministry, but that did not seem likely. Ministry required four years of undergraduate study and three years of seminary. Seven years of career preparation no longer seemed realistic.

Linda Andresen is Engaged

Starting our Life Together

My grief over not being able to return to Bethany was ameliorated when I reconnected with Linda Andresen. One evening that summer I stopped at her house to see how this old girlfriend and recent high school graduate was doing. I learned that she had recently ended a dating relationship with a steady boyfriend. Her availability delighted me and I asked her for a date that Saturday night. Within a short period, we became a couple.

That fall, I began attending Kent State full-time while continuing to work twenty hours per week at Kroger. Linda began to attend an Akron business school to learn to operate a comptometer, a ninety-nine key mechanical calculator. When she completed the course, she went to work at an Akron food wholesaler. Jobs, school and study kept us very busy. We saw each other as often as possible, but not nearly as often as we would have liked.

On March 7, 1962, Linda's nineteenth birthday, we announced our engagement and started to plan a summer wedding. In hindsight, there was no logical explanation for that. I was only twenty and still had two years of undergraduate school. Over the years, we have explained our decision by saying, "We decided to marry while we were young enough to think we had all the answers, but before we learned what the questions were going to be." More accurately, we deeply loved each other and getting married seemed like the thing to do— whether that was logical or not.

Family reaction was mixed. My mother voiced concerns that we were too young and if I married I would not finish my education. I assume John Strizak expected me to do something dumb like that. Neither my father nor the Andresens ever commented on how they felt. Leona seemed pleased for the extra space in the house. A few weeks after our wedding she eliminated my small bedroom in order to enlarge the living room.

After the wedding, we set up house in a small apartment over a double garage at 1960 Marhofer Road, Stow, Ohio. The rent was $35 per month. I continued to go to college and work at Kroger. Linda worked at the food distributor. We socialized with Joel and Pat Fischer as well as Denis and Gretchen Kuhlke, married friends from high school. We lived in that apartment until graduation from college.

August 25, 1962

For about six months I tried graduate school at Kent State. I quit the job at Kroger, became a graduate assistant in the biology department and took master's level courses in entomology and invertebrate physiology. My goal was to become a college biology professor, but the money ran short. It seemed a good idea to postpone school until the family treasury could be replenished. After interviewing for a number of Akron area jobs—including selling caskets to funeral homes, I tried the placement bureau at the university. They had an intriguing opportunity with the United States Public Health Service. On a whim, I scheduled an interview. Little did I know I was about to enter one of the most formative times in my life.

Leaving the Akron Area

The public health interview went very well. The job was for a federally funded project to eradicate early syphilis by interviewing infected patients for sexual contacts, finding those contacts and bringing them into the health department for examination and, if necessary, treatment. In addition to being offered a job as a VD investigator, I had a choice of working in New York City, Los Angeles or Detroit. Linda and I talked it over and decided on Detroit. It was only three hours from home. The other places seemed beyond our comfort zone.

I immediately went to the Motor City to find an apartment. At a get-acquainted stop at the Venereal Disease Clinic, the boss assigned Dave Claar to orient me to the city. As we got into his car, Dave said he had to make a stop. He drove into a ramshackle neighborhood that resembled parts of London after the Germans bombed. We stopped at what appeared to be an abandoned warehouse, walked down an alley and up a rickety staircase. Dave knocked on the door. A fellow answered and we entered a dimly lighted space crowded with people of all ages. Two bartenders worked a highly polished wooded bar serving drinks. Young women kept appearing and disappearing down an even darker hallway, holding the hands of men. In my capacity as a public health professional, I was to visit this place often in the months to come. It was called Tony's and it was the largest house of prostitution in Detroit.

A Serendipitous Friendship
Dave Claar and his wife, Ginny, became personal friends in Detroit. We have kept in touch over the years. Recently they moved to Cincinnati to be near a daughter and our old friendship was jumpstarted. What a blessing when old friends become close friends again.

After finishing a few weeks training at an inner city VD Clinic in Chicago, we moved to Detroit and settled into our new life. We quickly learned Detroit was as far beyond our comfort zone as we had feared New York and Los Angeles would be. Detroit auto plants dwarfed the tire factories of Akron. It was said that at Ford's River Rouge trains unloaded iron ore at one end of the factory and finished automobiles were loaded on trucks and trains at the other end. Even middle-of-the-night auto factory shift changes caused bumper-to-bumper traffic jams on Detroit's freeways. In addition, the racial and ethnic diversity of home paled in comparison. In the 1960s, half the residents of Detroit were African American. The Polish population in the enclave of Hamtramck was so dense that the neon signs on businesses were written in Polish. That was often the first language spoken in Hamtramck doctors' offices I visited.

Because things were different in the inner city, much was learned about the problems of race and poverty. In the neighborhood where Linda and I lived, trash collection was a regular occurrence. In the urban core it seemed a hit or miss proposition that resulted in significant accumulations of garbage in the alleys and streets. Feral dogs fed on the trash. Our apartment complex near suburban Dearborn was operated by an efficient and responsive management company. If we had a problem, we called and the problem was addressed. That was not necessarily so in the urban core.

One Saturday morning I paid a visit to a rundown tenement. I knocked on an apartment door in hopes the residents might know the person for whom I was looking. An elderly couple, probably in their seventies, invited me into their small apartment to discuss the matter. A delightful conversation ensued. Like many African Americans of their generation, they had moved from the Deep South in hopes of a better life in Detroit. Both had retired from a car wash. The job was not what they had hoped for, but it was still better than harvesting cotton in the Mississippi Delta. They served me a glass of iced tea in an old jelly jar. The woman apologized for not having real drinking glasses. As we chatted, I noticed a terrible smell. In a few minutes, yellow smoke started coming under the apartment door. The couple got up from the table and began to open windows and push towels under the door. They explained that their absentee landlord did not want to pay for a professional exterminator. Instead, he burned sulfur in the hallways. The wife explained that the sulfur did not kill roaches, but it made residents sick. I left that day recognizing that grandparents in my neighborhood would never be treated that way.

It is a different world for the poor and racial minorities. I make no claim to fully understand all the ways this is true, but my experiences with the U.S. Public Health Service provided an occasional peek into the world of others. I think those experiences made me a little more understanding, perhaps even a little less judgmental.

There were about twenty-five Federal VD investigators working in Detroit. Although we all worked with a wide range of people, each of us tended to develop a specialty, e.g., the prostitutes at Tony's, the gay community or even knowledge of a specific neighborhood. I specialized in working with a network of transvestite prostitutes, that is, men who dressed like women in order to sell their bodies to men who desired men dressed like women or as often happened, men who thought they were picking up a woman only to discover they were not. For the most part, my specialty group lived and worked in the same neighborhood. I could easily identify them as they walked the streets. These men were the best-dressed, best-looking women in the neighborhood.

I was eventually transferred to Grand Rapids where I worked with the health departments in ten to fifteen western Michigan counties. My VD investigations were mainly among migratory harvest workers, African-Americans from Florida and Braceros from central Mexico.

The Call to Ministry

Paul's call to ministry came as the resurrected Christ spoke to him in a dazzling light and loud voice on the Damascus Road. My call to ministry came in far less dramatic ways. Rather than struck temporarily blind, I believe God's called me with a series of tugs, nudges and encounters frequently not identified until years later.

To illustrate, I recall a conversation with a Detroit prostitute. She was a heroin addict and only sixteen years old. As we talked, I remember thinking of her as an unfortunate child overwhelmed by circumstances beyond her control. The major concern of her life should not be turning a trick in order to buy her next fix. She should be deciding what to wear to the school prom. She deserved better.

The plight of that young woman haunted me. By getting her examined and treated for a serious infectious disease I did something positive. That intervention, however, was too late to make a significant difference. In all likelihood she was going to have a very short, brutal life. I began to think about working at something that might offer a more holistic approach to human need.

In the years since, I have come to believe that the conversation with that young woman was one of those nudges toward ministry. God spoke to me, not in a blinding light on the Damascus Road, but in a dimly lit house of prostitution on Saint Antoine Street in Detroit. To paraphrase the song, "Surely the presence of the Lord was in that place."

The transfer to Grand Rapids also offered opportunities that in retrospect I have come to believe were also part of my call to ministry. A few weeks after we arrived in western Michigan we heard from Velma Workman, our Stow High history teacher. She informed us the uncle of Nannette Gaylord, a classmate of mine, was the minister at Cascade Christian Church in Grand Rapids. Miss Workman suggested we might visit that congregation

We were living on the far west side of the city and the church was on the far east side. Normally, we would not travel that far to church. We decided, however, to humor our former teacher and visit. We loved the church. Nice people. Good preacher. Raymond Gaylord, the minister, invited us to return and we did. Linda began to sing in the choir. I taught the sixth grade boys' Sunday School class and began to work with youth groups. Soon after joining, we learned that this Michigan congregation had been founded a hundred years previously by people from Stow, Ohio. In fact, the oldest graves in the Cascade Cemetery had many of the same names as our hometown cemetery.

One Sunday, the minister and his wife invited us to lunch. Raymond began talking about the congregation. The church and the community were growing rapidly. In order to sustain that growth, he needed help—particularly with youth and Christian Education. He said Velma Workman had told him I was once interested in ministry and he had come to the conclusion I would be the perfect person to be the congregation's first full-time Director of Youth and Education.

On first hearing that job offer did not seem particularly interesting. Linda and I assured Raymond, however, that we would talk about it. He said he didn't need an answer right away. The position was not going to be funded for several months.

We did think and talk about it—albeit not seriously. A more pressing matter took precedence. Linda was going to have a baby. We were overjoyed. On the other hand, we were clueless as to what was required of parents. This was particularly true for me. I can remember only three things I did to prepare: (1) I constantly thought about having a baby—usually with a big smile on my face. (2) I went with Linda to the hospital for three or four evening meetings on pregnancy, birth and parenting. After those classes, I thought I was fully prepared. (3) I sold a pint of my blood for $25. With that money, we purchased the layette—blankets, the initial bundle of diapers, etc.

Gender-predicting technology was limited at the time. Friends, relatives, even the nurse in the doctor's office told Linda she was carrying a baby boy. Consequently, we settled on the name, Stephen Vincent.

Imagine our surprise when Karen Marie was born April 1, 1966. The name was chosen because we liked the sound of it. As far as we knew, there was no other Karen or Marie in either family. Shortly after her birth, we returned to Stow to take our beloved firstborn on a grand tour of relatives. When we stopped to see Linda's paternal grandmother, Olga Andresen, she clapped her hands and cooed, "So this is Karen Marie, the little girl named after both of her great-great grandmothers!"

Olga and her husband Oluf had emigrated from Denmark about 1910. Apparently Karen Marie is a common name in Denmark. In fact, it is so common that the mothers of both Olga and Oluf had that name.

Three years later, on January 9, 1969, our other daughter was born. She too was predicted to be a son and we were going to name him Stephen Vincent. Instead, we settled on a much more appropriate name, Colleen Annette. As on the day Karen was born, Colleen's birth is remembered as one of those Holy Mountaintop Experiences of standing in the presence of God.

On Having Daughters

If a son had been born to us, I am sure I would have been pleased. However, I do not feel I missed anything by not having a son. Our daughters have been and continue to be absolutely wonderful. They brought me great joy when they were children and as adults I continue to marvel at their wisdom and accomplishments. Daughters have provided every benefit this father could have imagined or expected from being a parent, including choosing husbands whom I both love and admire as though they are my natural sons. It must also be noted that our daughters have given birth to and are in the process of raising our four absolutely wonderful grandchildren, Annie, Libby, Ben and Bryce.

Colleen and Karen

After that luncheon conversation and ministry invitation from Raymond Gaylord, he kept encouraging me toward ministry. He even asked me to preach the sermon during a Lenten service. Although obviously unplanned, Karen was born the day after I preached. Still we were, however, not thinking highly of the ministry opportunity.

Then the U.S. Public Health Service informed me I was to be transferred to an administrative position in Gary, Indiana. I did not want to work in administration and we did not want to move to Gary. Perhaps this job as Director of Youth and Christian Education could be a stopgap measure.

On July 1, 1966, I began what was expected to be a temporary foray into Christian ministry. At Cascade Christian, I worked with the youth groups, planned and administrated the congregation's Christian Education program and served as Pastoral Assistant to Rev. Gaylord by staffing committee meetings as well as making home and hospital visits.

While we were in Grand Rapids, we were also introduced to church camp at Crystal Lake. To convince a reluctant wife to spend a week at family camp in an aging moldy cabin, I promised to buy a kitchen table, chairs and a buffet. That buffet remains in our Lexington basement. At the time, Karen was fifteen months old. To take care of her needs, we tied her baby bed and high chair to the top of the car. It took an hour to scrub the dead bugs from Karen' furniture at the end of each leg of the trip. That and a host of similar experiences provide wonderful memories of going to Crystal Lake.

After a year at the church, I came to realize I really enjoyed ministry. I started attending Western Theological Seminary in Holland, Michigan. I usually took one or two classes each term and the church paid for books and tuition. Western is a Seminary of the Reformed Church in America, a predominantly Dutch expression of Protestantism that first came to America in the Seventeenth Century. As orthodox Calvinists, their theological stance differed significantly from the Christian Church (Disciples of Christ), but students were welcoming and the professors gracious. Since my name is Swiss and not Dutch, they may have appreciated the ethnic diversity I brought to an otherwise homogenous student body.

The classes were interesting and meaningful, but I was not always certain how useful they were. In response, Raymond and I began regular discussions of the practical implications of what seminary teaches. I owe a great thanks to Raymond for mentoring me into ministry.

Of course, Raymond's lessons were not all on point. For instance, Ray spent so much time at church he neglected his family. Because he was my role model, I began to spend so much time at the church that I neglected my wife and child. Fortunately, Providence intervened. I signed up for an evening seminary class on Marriage and Family Counseling in Fall 1968.

The professor, a particularly wise man, required all students to bring their spouses or significant others.

Each week that term, Linda and I hired a babysitter to watch Karen and drove forty-five miles to class. We sat next to each other for the three-hour class. Then we drove another forty-five miles home. This afforded a taste of the quality time that Linda and I needed. We talked all the way from Grand Rapids to Holland on the general topics we had been neglecting since Karen's birth. At the conclusion of the class, we talked from Holland to Grand Rapids on topics raised in class and how those topics applied to our marriage and family. It was a wonderful experience.

I make no claim that all notions of ministry as hard work were expunged from my pastoral practices. I still believe many weaknesses can be overcome by working harder, smarter and longer. I have also learned, however, that to be effective in ministry, a married pastor cannot neglect spouse and family. From that point on, I tried to find some balance between work and family.

In early January 1969, a couple of months after that class ended, our younger daughter indicated readiness to make her family debut. Linda began to have labor pains. They were not severe, were separated by about ten minutes and lasted thirty to forty seconds. We waited for the pains to get closer and become more severe, but it didn't happen. The doctor called it unproductive labor and claimed it was caused by the winter's low barometric pressure. He also told us this could last for days.

Ordinarily, I would have continued my routine of going to work regardless of circumstances at home. If this was going to take days, I had things that needed to be done. I normally would have reasoned that Linda could call me when she needed a ride to the hospital. Because of the commitment to be a more present husband, I stayed home. In fact, I did not go to work for three or four days while Linda was in this unproductive stage of labor. This does not seem like much, but at the time, it marked a change in my attentiveness.

When Colleen was born on January 9, 1969, it felt as though the heavens opened and the earth moved. What a blessing to participate in the creation of life. What a miraculous event. What a wonderful child.

A Ministry Story

A Presbyterian minister colleague says he has a recurring dream in which he attends his own funeral. His wife and children are sitting in the front row at the gravesite. They are unaware he watches the proceedings from behind them. As the service ends, the funeral director presents his wife with a box of the appointment calendars her husband had accumulated over forty years in ministry. This husband/father/minister peers over his wife's shoulder as she thumbs through the calendars. He is struck by how often he was working at the church on not particularly significant things when he could have just as easily been home with the family. He glances up at his own tombstone. His epitaph has already been inscribed: "Daddy has gone to another church meeting."

I never had that dream, but I identify with it. Sometimes I wonder how nice it would be to know earlier in life some of what we come to know by end of life.

The Move to Indiana

By the end of three years at Cascade Church, it became apparent that this temporary foray into ministry was likely to be long term. I had completed about half the course work for a Master of Divinity degree and realized if I was going to be a Disciple minister I needed to finish my studies where there were other Disciple students and professors.

By this time, we had two children, a house full of furniture and a $60 per month car payment. We decided to look for a Disciple-related seminary where we could serve a student church and live in a parsonage while accruing as little debt as possible. We settled on Christian Theological Seminary because Bill Barnes, the school's Vice-President for Development, convinced us CTS best met out needs. Bill was right. We fit well with what CTS had to offer.

Our student church was in Springport, Indiana, about fifty miles from the seminary. The town consisted of about seventy-five houses, two hundred people and a wide assortment of stray dogs on an intersection of two county roads, a mile off a state highway. The church was the biggest building in town and the parsonage was the newest house. The post office, a building with clapboard siding and 150 square feet of floor space, was the morning gathering place for retired farmers waiting to greet residents stopping for the day's mail. Cecil Sellers, the postmaster, was quick to defend his humble workplace. "The flag atop this building is just like the one that flies over the White House in Washington D.C."

Each day Linda bundled Karen and Colleen into a little red wagon and pulled them down the hill to pick up the mail. She put so many miles with that wagon the handle wore off and was replaced by a piece of clothes line. What remains of the wagon is stored in our basement. We have yet to decide its fate. Perhaps we will bequeath it to the Disciple Historical Society as a museum display on what life was like for seminary student spouses in the second half of the twentieth century.

Many of the people in the Springport area made their living as family farmers. The primary crops were corn and soybeans. Most farmers also raised chickens, dairy or beef cattle as well as hogs. To the Cuenis, Springport farmers seemed especially fond of hogs. We estimated about 2,000 pigs were within a mile of the parsonage. No matter the wind direction, one was aware of their presence. When Naomi Rutherford was queried as to how she tolerated the hog smell in her farm kitchen, she responded, "That just smells like money to me."

The farmers of Springport Christian Church offered a wonderful corrective to this young man's confidence in the powers of self-determination. Growing up around factory workers, coal miners, urban and suburban people, I was led to believe personal decisions chart our fate. "Decide what you want to do and do it." "Work hard and you will get ahead. If you are not getting ahead, work even harder." "Pull yourself up by your own bootstraps."

In Springport, I was shown the limits of those ideas. Farming requires making rational business decisions. Farmers must take responsibility for themselves. They must work hard. Their success, however, is not totally in their control. They still must depend on rain in the right amounts and at the right time. They need the right soil temperature during the planting season and good market prices. Over those and a number of other variables, they have no control. Farmers can only do their best. Then they must wait and see.

In Springport I met farm people who lived with a dynamic tension between self-determination and acquiescence to circumstances beyond their control. This instilled in them a sense of acceptance, patience and peace about the conduct of life that I had not experienced in non-farm people. It was an important lesson.

The Springport congregation had been a student church for well over a half-century. Because they called new student ministers every two to four years, they understood the proper nurture and care of an inexperienced pastor. Roscoe Bell chaired the search committee that called me and became one of my mentors for about ten years. I well remember walking into one of my first board meetings. Roscoe pulled me aside and said, "The church owns five acres on the edge of town. The farmers take turns planting and harvesting that field. Today we decide who is going to do the work this year. This conversation often degenerates to an argument. Since you do not own farm equipment and will not be taking a turn, I suggest you not comment. You will discover that silence will be more helpful than speaking." That advice was regularly applied over the next thirty-five years.

Sunday morning attendance at Springport Christian Church was fifty to seventy-five. The choir had eight to ten members. Nineteenth century Gospel dominated the hymn choices. Nearly everyone who came to worship also came to Sunday School. The all-church pitch-in dinners were both regular and glorious events. The fried chicken was always presented in an iron skillet. The buffet line vegetables were still in cooking pans. I came to think the food was delicious because the first sentence on farm house recipes was "Take a spoon of lard."

In addition to preaching every Sunday, I taught the high school Sunday School class. The second year in Springport, Linda cleaned the church for $10 per week and I mowed the church-owned cemetery for $2 per hour. The extra money helped. I also came to love being a local church pastor even more deeply.

Three days each week I drove back and forth between Springport and the Seminary. To finish in two years, I needed to take ten to twelve hours for credit each semester. I especially enjoyed courses in Church History, Theology of Ecology, Bio-Medical Ethics, Theology of Rudolf Bultmann, Theology of Thomas Aquinas and The Work and Person of Christ.

After taking a speech course entitled, Forms of Public Address for the Minister, the professor asked me to be his teaching assistant. This was a great opportunity to hone my public speaking skills and the job paid $350 per semester. The extra money came in handy.

Other than taking classes, I did not get involved with school activities. I had a family, was a church pastor and lived an hour from campus. Spare time was limited. Christian Theological Seminary was, however, a great academic and intellectually enriching experience. I have always been grateful for a seminary education.

In September 1970, Eric White, the Michigan Regional Minister, called me to say the minister in Petoskey was going to retire. He wondered if I might be interested in being considered for the job. We had not given much thought to where we wanted to go, but we had liked Michigan and told him we were open to talking with Petoskey, even though we knew nothing of the church or the community.

An interview was arranged for October, at the height of autumn color. Friends cared for our children while Linda and I drove north. We were growing weary of the drive when Linda, the family navigator, looked at the map and said, "I think we are about there." A few minutes later, she said, "Oh, no! There is another fold in the map. We still have a few more hours." At that point, we decided we were not interested in going to Petoskey. It was too isolated, too far from family in Ohio, too far north, and just too cold.

As we continued north, we saw billboards advertising the city. We learned Petoskey had Montgomery Ward and J.C. Penney stores. Then we saw a billboard claiming Petoskey as the smallest city in America to have a branch of Saks Fifth Avenue. Obviously this was a different type of small, isolated community. Maybe it was even a special place.

After a long, long drive from rural Indiana, we reached our destination. From the top of the hill, we saw a magnificent little community nestled around the shore of the Little Traverse

Bay. The sun was low in the west. The fall colors were at their height. It was one of the most beautiful sights I had ever seen. I looked at Linda and said, "Maybe we should take this seriously. This looks like a great place to raise children."

Two days later we had decided that after graduation, we were going to move to northern Michigan. We returned to Springport, to seminary and to the routine that had become our lives. It was going to be eight months before I graduated and we moved north.

4

Petoskey and Life after Seminary

As I moved through seminary, I struggled with whether or not to be ordained. I was unconvinced of ordination's importance or necessity. Historically the Christian Church (Disciples of Christ) was a movement of laity. Almost from the beginning we had ministers, but their role and how they differed from the congregation's membership was fuzzy. Unlike the Roman Catholic Church, we did not consider ordination a sacrament, nor did we think our ministers had any unique access to God. Unlike most Protestant denominations, the Disciples never reserved any function of ministry for the ordained. Technically any member of the church could serve communion, chair the governing board, preach and do funerals. As is still said from time to time, "The Disciples have ministers. What we do not have are lay people. Every member of the church is a minister."

By seminary graduation, I had been serving in ministry for five years. I had been pastor at Springport for two years. I was a Licensed Minister in the Christian Church (Disciples of Christ). That permitted me to park in the clergy parking spots at the hospital. Why did I need to be ordained?

With encouragement from people I respected, I decided to be ordained if I could write the liturgy for the service. I wanted ordination vows to be consistent with my theology of ministry. I was given that opportunity and was ordained to be a faithful servant of the Christ, called by God and confirmed by the Church with the responsibility of seeing that the various functions of the church's ministry were performed. The vows I wrote insisted I was not a leader with the last word on matters of faith, doctrine, mission and ministry. I was ordained as a minister in an egalitarian covenant with all members of the church.

On Being Ordained
Today Disciple polity does not permit a candidate for ordination to write his or her ordination vows. Within a few years of my ordination, Disciples adopted a more formal/structured understanding of the office of Ordained Minister that fits more congenially with historic Mainline Protestant views. The distinctiveness of ministry among Disciples common when I began is no more.

Ministry on *the Shores of Gitchigumi* *by the Shining Big Sea Waters*

This abbreviated quotation comes from Nathaniel Hawthorne's epic poem, *Hiawatha*. The poet is assumed to be referring to the shore of Lake Superior, but I contend the shore of Lake Michigan is close enough for a good story.

Two weeks after ordination, an Allied Moving van found its way to Springport, Indiana, loaded all our household goods and took them to Petoskey, Michigan, a city of about 7,000 nestled on the south shore of Lake Michigan's Little Traverse Bay. Workers unloaded the truck into what was to become our family home for the next six-and-a-half years.

The First Christian Church parsonage was separated from the church only by a narrow driveway. Before we installed a curtain for privacy, Linda often noticed the church secretary standing at her office window, benignly staring into our home, watching Linda and the kids going about daily life.

It was a rambling old house with an overabundance of downstairs rooms. In addition to a living room, dining room, kitchen, and full bath, the downstairs also had a snow/mud foyer between the front door and the storm door for kicking weather off of shoes and boots, a television room with French doors to separate it from the living room, a cedar-lined walk-in closet almost the size of a small bedroom, a walk-in pantry with sufficient shelf space for more groceries than we could afford, a walk-through hallway and storage space between the living room and the bathroom that was so convoluted that two-and-a-half-year-old Colleen once wandered in, could not find her way out, sat down and shouted, "Mom help me. I'm lost."

In addition, the downstairs had two rooms for which names had to be invented. The Cold Room was the size of the average apartment living room. The name came from the fact it had no insulation in the outside wall. In the winter its temperature always approached freezing. The Toy Room was as large as the living room. The name came from deep, built-in shelves on one wall where the children's toys were stored.

The downstairs bathroom was an architectural anomaly. It could be entered through three different doors. To insure privacy, all three had to be securely closed and locked. Unfortunately by the time that was accomplished, one risked being too late. The kitchen was both pleasant and enormous. The dish cupboards posed the only serious problem. They hung on outer, poorly insulated walls. During winter months, the dishes had to be heated in the oven or on the furnace air grates before food could be served.

While the downstairs was architecturally diverse and interesting, the upstairs was rather ordinary. Its only charming feature was a long, curving staircase. Linda regularly permitted our daughters to ride down those stairs in a plastic laundry basket. As might be anticipated, this practice required frequent replacement of laundry baskets.

I have great family memories of living in the house. Karen started kindergarten and went into sixth grade there. Colleen went from a toddler to early third grade. Linda finished the intense years of mothering and began to have a little personal time. Linda and I had faithfully kept a Friday date night since Colleen was an infant. In Petoskey, the girls got to the point that we could leave them alone for a short time so we could take a walk—just to talk. It was a good time, indeed.

We arrived on the shores of Gitchigumi late in June 1971. The church had just celebrated its seventy-fifth anniversary. I was twenty-nine years old, had spent five years taking classes in seminary and had been employed by the Church of Jesus Christ

Petoskey, Michigan

for five years. This is to say that neither the congregation nor its pastor were novices in ministry. We should have known what we were doing. It was not that simple.

My much loved predecessor retired from the congregation after a seventeen-year ministry. The last ten years he had used much of his time and energy building a retirement home on Torch Lake, about fifty miles to the south. For a decade, his ministerial responsibilities had been limited to hospital calls and preaching on Sunday. The congregation knew their pastor needed a place to retire and were glad to provide the time. This meant, however, that for a decade, the congregation had drifted. They had no plan, no vision, no effective organizational structure and no program, other than Sunday School, worship, potluck dinners and an annual county fair fundraiser. The congregation was not troubled by this. On the contrary, they were happy as a chorus of clams. Consequently they had few expectations for the new minister beyond maintaining the status quo.

While true that I had worked as a congregational minister for five years, the programmatic and administrative buck had never stopped with me. At Cascade, Ray Gaylord took the responsibility. The congregation's ministry at Springport was limited to Sunday School, worship, the annual Ice Cream Social and an occasional Pitch-in Dinner. For decades, the Springport Church saw their primary ministry as nurturing student pastors.

As their current project, they expected me only to visit the sick, preach on Sunday, attend seminary during the week and do an occasional wedding or funeral.

The Petoskey ministry routine took a few months to establish. I worked my plan for getting acquainted, set aside fifteen to twenty hours for weekly sermon preparation, visited hospitalized members daily and taught a Sunday School class for younger adults.

By the third month I easily handled the workload. By the fourth month, I was bored and needed more to do. I began to ask experienced ministers how they filled their time. Most were simply puzzled by my question. They served congregations of the same size and did not get everything done. They could not identify with my boredom.

Fortunately, some colleagues understood and made helpful suggestions. One colleague advised me to enrich congregational life with short-term educational experiences. He told me these events should be more than the generic Christian Education opportunities touted in local Christian bookstores. Meaningful Christian education opportunities must be tailored to fit the culture and needs of the particular congregation.

Since there had been a paucity of adult education experiences during the past decade, I began to do a weekday morning Bible and Theology Study. This was advertised as a study that took the faith seriously by helping people think through what they really believed. Rather than imposing my agenda on the class, we discussed questions of the attendees. The format generated great conversation and, hopefully, growth in the faith of the participants.

I also began to ponder the approaching northern Michigan winter. People had warned us that winters were not only long and physically demanding, but psychologically draining. Each winter averaged eight to ten feet of snow. Due to what is called Lake Effect, a full month or six weeks might pass without seeing the sun. People, particularly the elderly and stay-at-home mothers, spent an inordinate amount of time in the house, behind closed doors, isolated from others and without benefit of sunshine. Weeks would often pass without the temperature rising above freezing. These weather conditions gave rise to a widespread existential dis-ease called Cabin Fever.

I responded to this malady by planning a series of Sunday evening all-church fellowship and learning events collectively called Cabin Fever College. The objective was to give the congregation an opportunity to get out the house, to come together as a faith community, and perhaps to think, to learn, and to grow in the faith. In addition to snacks, child care and fellowship, I prepared a lesson for the adults on some topic of general interest. The format of Cabin Fever College was sufficiently meaningful to continue at pastorates in Bedford, Indiana, as well as Bloomington, Illinois.

What I Had Yet to Learn about Leadership
While in Petoskey I came face to face with what seminary had not and really could not teach me about ministerial leadership. I did not know how to tease possibilities, hopes and dreams out of the congregation; how to weave threads of ideas into a tapestry that could be held before the congregation as something they identified as their vision for the future; how to build a consensus; and how to develop a plan, recruit and train people to get involved. Those lessons and skills would take years to learn.

Another colleague listened to my laments about being bored and encouraged community involvement. A congregation the size of Petoskey, he told me, simply was never going to keep me as busy as I wanted to be. I needed to connect with the wider community.

I took this advice and began volunteering as an assistant coach on a flag football team of fifth and sixth Grade boys. I had a wonderful time. The team went undefeated and outscored the opposition 240–6. This success had little to do with the skills of this inexperienced assistant coach. Several years later, many of the stars at Petoskey High School, including the quarterback and most of the other skill positions, had played on that flag football team. Talented players tend to make inadequate coaching look good.

I also got involved with a group of young adults who were trying to address a growing problem of drug abuse. This was the early 1970s. The Anti-Vietnam War Counter-Culture

Hippy Movement was in full swing and recreational drug use was rampant. Particularly during the summer, the downtown city park was crowded with curiously clothed, long-haired, slightly odiferous, on-the-road young adults. Many of this group saw a different meaning in a chemical company slogan popular at the time: *Better Living Through Chemistry.*

A small number from the Counter-Culture had become alarmed at the damage being done by widespread drug use. They wanted to find a way to address the problem. I assume they needed some non-hippy young adult to bring credibility to their task because I was invited to join them. It turned out to be a rather successful endeavor. We applied to the state of Michigan for funding. When the state responded positively, we established an agency that employed a couple of drug counselors. Eventually that agency became part of the Emmet Country Mental Health Clinic. When it did, I was invited to be on the board of directors for the ECMHC and eventually became board president.

These added activities kept me much busier, but did not resolve my underlying sense of boredom. From this I learned three things: (1) The problem had more to do with me than the job. I am not content simply to be busy. I like to be overly busy. (2) I need to be meaningfully engaged, not just busy. I find joy in solving a problem, mastering a new skill or facing a challenge. (3) The tendency to become bored has kept me intellectually and spiritually curious. On the other hand, it is a frustration that has nipped at my heels most of my ministry.

Discovering Two Ministry Passions

While in Petoskey I began to write for publication and to develop a keen interest in developing healthy marriages. These activities were important at each of my ministry sites as well as sources of enormous satisfaction.

That I would find enjoyment in writing seems incongruous with my growing-up years. In elementary school I demonstrated no particular gift in language arts. In junior high the teacher's diagramed sentences made as much sense as instructions on nuclear fission. My objective was to survive high school English, not learn from it. As a college freshman, English was my least favorite class. When I transferred to Kent State, I was mandated to the remedial composition course. Through undergraduate school, I showed no particular promise for developing an idea and expressing it on paper.

When I started seminary, I learned this was going to be a problem. As an undergraduate biology major the longest paper I had written was eight pages, mostly of graphs and charts. Seminary professors expected at least one and sometimes two twenty-five- to thirty-page papers for every course. During five years of seminary, I not only learned to write; I discovered I enjoyed it.

In Petoskey, I began to write a weekly essay/meditation for the front page of the church newsletter. Doing so provided an opportunity to let the creative juices flow. Little did I know the importance of those brief articles.

Soon after my arrival, Harold Kohn phoned me. He invited me to visit him at his home in Charlevoix, sixteen miles to the west. I needed no further encouragement. I had heard about Harold, a well-known naturalist, inspirational speaker, pastoral counselor, congregational minister, artist, and author. He was a living legend in northern Michigan and I was thrilled for the opportunity to meet him.

During that visit, Harold told me he was on our congregation's newsletter mailing list and had been impressed by my articles. He thought I needed a wider audience and should begin to publish. At that time, Harold was a regular contributor to Sunday's *Parade* magazine and the monthly *Reader's Digest,* both read by millions. He was the author of a dozen books, primarily collections of essays on faith and the natural world. As an artist, he illustrated his own books. I thought, "If he thinks I have the ability to publish, I should pay attention."

Harold spent much of that visit sharing his wisdom on how a congregational minister could break into publishing. He stressed lessons on Locating the Right Publisher, Avoiding the Discouragement of Rejection, and Understanding Writing as an Extension of Ministry, Not an Avenue to Wealth.

I went home, followed his directions, heeded his precautions and began to submit articles for publication. I frequently communicated with Harold. He was always gracious and helpful. In time, an occasional acceptance interrupted the steady stream of rejections. At first I was merely thrilled to see my name in print. In time, writing for publication became an important way to enrich my life and ministry.

That initial visit with Harold Kohn set in motion a friendship and mentoring relationship that continued until his death. I treasure his memory. The intersecting of our lives was, for me, another of those Holy Encounters.

The source of my interest in developing healthy marriages is not as easily identified. It may have simply originated in a concern that my own marriage not become as problematic as those I experienced as a child. Whatever the genesis, improving marriages became a ministry passion. I have researched the topic extensively, wrote a doctoral dissertation/project on marriage counseling theories, programmed marriage enrichment opportunities in every congregation I served and developed a reputation as an effective marriage counselor. I have seen nothing that causes me to disagree with D.H. Lawrence when he called marriage the center of human life.

I began doing marriage counseling in northern Michigan soon after arriving. The first couple with whom I worked were members of the congregation. They were pregnant with their first child and she was threatening divorce. They told me they came to me because they thought their new minister might be helpful. They did not know my only formal preparation was that seminary class in Marriage and Family Counseling.

Fortunately, nothing was organically wrong with their relationship. She was pregnant. Her body was changing. Her hormones were raging. She didn't know what to do about her strange feelings and thoughts other than to threaten divorce. I talked with them about six or seven times. I got them to discuss how each felt about this baby and to face their apprehensions that their lives were going to change. They reassured each other about their ongoing love. They reconciled, went away happy, had that child and then a couple more. To my knowledge they remained married.

I make no claim for having contributed much to this process. After all, I didn't know enough to make a meaningful contribution. However, this couple told their friends about the new minister in town who helped them. The word spread and others began to make appointments.

A small practice emerged as a steady stream of couples started coming to see me. They represented a cross-section from a blue collar couple in their fifties who commuted more than a hundred miles each way on icy winter roads to a prominent local physician and his wife. Most counselees, however, were young adults who found marriage more difficult than anticipated.

Initially, I was puzzled by the growing popularity. It was not as if I was counseling primarily parishioners. Most of my clientele came from the community. Few expressed interest in the theological dimensions of their relationship. Even though I did not charge, money could not have been the reason. For the needy, trained professionals at the mental health clinic offered free therapy. I had read a couple of books and had taken one seminary class. Why would people come to an untrained, un-licensed minister/counselor when professional therapists were available?

Over time, several couples shared that they had gone to a professional therapist before coming to see me. Their experiences had not been particularly helpful. They explained further that what I was doing with them was different. This led me to wonder if marital counseling substantially differs from other forms of counseling. Perhaps a person untrained in psycho-therapy can be good at marriage counseling because marriage counseling is not, per se, psychotherapy.

Although I never dug deeply into the issue, I have con-cluded that what I did was more an educational pastoral ac-tivity than psychotherapy. My method, stated as succinctly as possible, followed this pattern.

(a) We started by discussing the relationship's positives rath-er than with the problems. Instead of giving the impression that marriage is a problem to solve, I wanted the couple to develop a sense their marriage was worth saving.

(b) Before getting to problem resolution, I asked them to decide if they wanted this relationship to improve or not. If they had already made up their minds to divorce, I needed to know that. Expecting to divorce can easily become a self-fulfilling prophecy. On the other hand, it is amazing how much effort people will put into a relationship when they are truly committed to making it work.

(c) We worked on framing the descriptions of the problems in ways that made it possible to resolve them. For instance, one couple insisted the root of their problem was ethnic origins. As the husband put it, "My family is German. Her family is Irish. The Germans and the Irish just don't get along." I assured them that while that might or might not be true, we could not change German-ness and Irish-ness. We needed to find ways to talk about perceived shortcomings that made it possible to correct them.

(d) Once they described what troubled them in a resolvable way, we began to look for what changes each thought would make a positive difference in their marriage. Often this required a little education on the reality of living in an imperfect world with an imperfect spouse. Every problem was not going to have a solution. Our humanness requires learning to live with a certain amount of irritation. This was all prelude to making an agreed-upon plan for changes that would make each partner feel more loved, appreciated and valued.

I do not really know if professional psychotherapists would agree with my approach to marriage counseling or not. It was, however, my way of doing things and it seemed to be helpful. Regardless, that's my story and I am sticking with it.

The Great Family Adventure

Five years into the Petoskey tenure, I got the itch to pursue a Doctor of Ministry degree. Although not enthusiastically encouraging, Linda was reluctantly willing. Mostly, she rolled her eyes at my educational restlessness.

In order to keep family disruption to a minimum, I looked for a doctoral program that would permit us to remain in Petoskey, not require me to be away from home for extended periods, be sufficiently inexpensive not to become a financial burden, and permit me to further develop my twin passions in ministry—writing and building healthier marriages.

San Francisco Theological Seminary fit every requirement. They put great emphasis on writing an extended dissertation/ project. They permitted each student to choose the topic, and I could write on some aspect of marriage. They had an off-campus group forming at Michigan's Alma College, about 120 miles south of Petoskey. This group was to meet each Monday for one year. I could drive down and back without being away overnight. Additionally, the entire family was encouraged to attend a summer residency in San Francisco. Total tuition was $2,000 and the board of First Christian Church agreed to pay this fee as well as provide me a paid sabbatical to study in San Francisco.

The family prepared for that sojourn for an entire year. We calculated that if we drove to California and back, the travel and incidental expenses beyond my salary would be about $1000. This meant living on a daily travel budget of $50 for food, gas, motel and incidental expenses. The remainder would cover additional living expenses in California. Thanks to having finished the payments on our old car and the discipline of squirreling away every spare dollar, we saved exactly $1,000 that year.

Living on a Less-Than-Adequate Income

In preparation for the trip, Linda and I applied for and received our first Visa bankcard. Prior to that, we had only charge cards that could be used in specific places or for specific items, e.g., J.C. Penney and Standard Oil. With a Visa, we could charge motels, food and gas. That, we reasoned, would be convenient on our trip. Of course, keeping the Visa after the trip made it possible for us to live ever so slightly beyond our means. This left us to struggle with the credit card bill later.

From the time our children were born until they were nearly in high school, we lived at the outer edge of our means. We saved next to nothing and lived from paycheck to paycheck. We never went without food, clothing or the basic necessities. We never spent money lavishly or foolishly. We never faulted on a debt and were never late on a payment. For many years, however, we struggled to make ends meet.

Two factors were behind this problem: (1) I simply did not make enough money to provide the family with a comfortable living. (2) Linda was a stay-at-home mother until our daughters were in late elementary and middle school. Only when we felt they were sufficiently independent did she go to work and contribute money to the family budget.

We could have corrected our income problem either by me changing to a profession that paid better than ministry or by Linda finding outside employment. We chose not to do either. Both of our mothers worked outside the home. Consequently, Linda spent a lot of time alone in the house waiting for her mother to come home. John Strizak was my childhood caregiver. I would have preferred to be alone. We wanted our children to have something we did not have—the assurance of a caring parent's presence when they came home from play or school.

Occasionally I considered leaving ministry for a more lucrative profession but could never think of anything else I wanted to do. For that matter, I had doubts that satisfaction in life could be found by making more money. As strange as it may seem, that notion came from a Collier's Magazine article I read in junior high while waiting for a turn in the barber's chair. The article reported on a study of people who earned from $4,000 per year (about average) to what I thought an unbelievable income of $25,000 per year. Almost every person in the study reported needing a little more money to make ends meet. Ironically, no matter the income bracket, the vast majority surveyed needed another $1,000 annually. From that I concluded that it really didn't matter how much money I made, we would still need just a little more.

A week prior to Karen and Colleen finishing fourth and first grades, we headed to California. We went in a newly purchased, three-year-old, full-sized Chrysler. It was family adventure perfect. With the addition of a borrowed car-top carrier, it held everything we needed.

We drove west across the Upper Peninsula of Michigan, through southern Minnesota and into South Dakota and Wyoming, headed south to Salt Lake City, then west through Nevada and into California. Among other places, we visited the Black Hills, Mount Rushmore and Yellowstone Park. One night we stopped in a small town in Nevada where we purchased a gallon of milk at a combination convenience market, slot machine emporium and porno magazine shop. The girls noticed the magazines before we could direct them to a less risqué aisle. Those magazines provoked endless questions that night.

The journey was close to idyllic. The scenery was magnificent. The car performed reliably. The family proved to be congenial travelers. It was a slight concern that we had to stop to fill the gas tank every 180 miles, but that was not a terrible problem. We often paid only thirty-five to forty cents per gallon.

It took five days to arrive in San Anselmo, where San Francisco Seminary is located. The school moved to this suburb after the 1906 earthquake. Upon our arrival we moved into the assigned apartment in married student housing and began meeting those with whom we were to live for the next six weeks. In addition to our Michigan group, there were groups from Florida, Georgia, and southern California.

During the year our group met weekly at Alma College, I came to realize that the experiences, expertise, faith journeys and personhoods of others in the class were as beneficial to learning as the contributions of the professors. The interactions of students and professors were stimulating both spiritually and intellectually. The San Francisco Seminary experience continued that and took it to an even higher level.

Some people I met in Alma and San Francisco served not only as role models for ministry, but as inspirations for abundant living. The most memorable were Jim and Edie Bell. She was a delightful person who contributed warmth, charm and grace to all she met. Edie was an accomplished watercolorist who painted several hours each day and sold her work from her own gallery. She gave Linda a landscape of San Francisco's Strawberry Point that still hangs in our home. Jim was a thoughtful, wise and kind member of our Alma group. Before coming to Michigan, he worked at his denomination's headquarters in an office that provided life-long learning opportunities for clergy. When he left that job to become an Executive Presbyter in Michigan he set a goal to finish a Doctor of Ministry degree before he retired. At the time, Linda and I were in our middle thirties. Jim and Edie were in their early sixties. Most of the people we had known in our growing-up years assumed it was necessary to slow down in the later years of life. Jim and Edie were inspirational role models for keeping on keeping on. They followed the wish of the anonymous poet, "Let me die working.

Clean to the end. Swift may my race be run." Thirty-five years later Linda and I are using the Bell's approach to growing older. Keep going as long as the body and mind permit. It feels good.

For the first four weeks in San Anselmo I was deeply immersed in classes, study and reading. Other than attending a different church each Sunday, there was little time with the family. Studies were less demanding the last two weeks and we had the opportunity to see the area. In addition to frequent afternoons getting acquainted with the city, we visited Alcatraz; gawked our way through Haight-Asbury, the neighborhood credited with having given birth to the drug culture and the Hippy movement; checked out Paul Masson winery; and negotiated Lombard, said to be the most crooked street in the world. Karen attended a San Francisco Giants baseball game with new friends. Colleen, who was just learning to read, practiced her developing skill by reading signs aloud as we toured the city. Although pleased with her reading progress, we were less than thrilled when, as we drove through a somewhat seedy neighborhood, she read aloud, "The Bare Your Ass Bar." We had a wonderful time in San Francisco.

From my perspective, this great family adventure was all I had hoped for. The extended family time was sublime and the educational experience was enriching. At the end of six weeks, however, we were ready to leave. We took the shortest possible route home to Petoskey in time to enjoy what little remained of the summer.

Winters in Petoskey

Before moving north, we knew that winters would be harder and longer than we had experienced in more southern climes. We had failed, however, to grasp the significance of how much longer and harder. That deficiency was quickly addressed. Within a few weeks of arriving, we were invited to a get-together of fifteen to twenty church members at John and Marilyn Emshwiller's house. The group thought the new minister and his family might appreciate a photographic presentation of various church activities. After the fourth or fifth slide showing heavily bundled children playing in banks of snow, I asked

"What are the kids doing?" Shirley Burgess responded, "That is last year's Easter Egg Hunt."

As I recall, Petoskey received 186 inches of snow our first winter. Toward the middle or end of March it was still snowing and I commented to Fred Friend, the octogenarian church custodian, about the amount of snow. He said, "Yes, this has been a hard winter, but this is above average. I can remember winters in which we only got 100 inches." Sorry, Fred, eight feet is still a lot of white stuff.

During Petoskey winters, I would learn: (1) Blowing snow from the parsonage driveway and church's sidewalks took about one hour, three or four days each week. (2) On a windy day, parked next to a snow bank, the family automobile can become completely buried. One should not despair. An automobile can be located in a snow bank by probing with a broom stick. (3) By putting snowshoes on one's feet, it is possible to walk on top of the snow. (4) In rural areas of northern Michigan, a snowmobile is the winter's most reliable form of transportation. Some days, it is the only transportation. (5) When the temperature hits 35 below zero, the house makes a curious, high-pitched sound. (6) By January, snow in intersections is sufficiently deep that precautions must be taken. To make one's automobile more visible tie a flag or streamer at the end of the car's radio antenna. In the absence of a radio antenna, tape a long stick to the side of the car with a flag fastened to it. (7) By the middle of February, snow in the parsonage front yard is sufficiently deep that Monroe Street could be seen only from bedroom windows on the second floor.

When we interviewed for the job in Petoskey, the Search Committee assured us that even though the winter was longer and harder, we would get used to it. We learned that was true. The winters were harder and longer. As predicted, we also grew accustomed to winter. However, there is a difference between growing accustomed to winter and liking it.

On September 20, 1976, about two months after returning from the Great Family Adventure, I came home for lunch. It was snowing on the last day of summer. I said to Linda, "The weather looks as though we might miss autumn this year and go directly to winter. I dread even that possibility. When we went to California I made a commitment to the congregation that we would stay one year. It will take at least a year to find a new place to do ministry, but I want this to be our last winter."

5

Becoming Hoosiers Again

Early in March, 1977, six months after deciding to move, Linda and I drove to Lansing to see the Michigan Regional Minister. We needed information on how the ministerial relocation process worked. He was both gracious and helpful.

Immediately after returning home, I completed the required forms, solicited references, and wrote an essay on my interest in finding a congregation that was theologically and personally compatible as well as pastorally challenging.

When completed, the forms were mailed to the proper office in Indianapolis where copies were to be distributed across the country. The Regional Minister had assured once my papers were in circulation, congregations would begin to call. In the meantime I fantasized about doing ministry in an exciting city with a mild winter at a well-paying congregation, housed in a beautiful facility with minimal or no debt, bustling with committed congregants ready to challenge the new pastor.

It was two months before the first call. Then a floodgate of inquiries opened. Twenty-six congregations called in a few weeks. Two-thirds of the contacts were from very nice people on search committees in churches or locations that did not match our needs or interests. There were, of course, inquiries that got our attention. A suburban Kansas City congregation was large, challenging and offered a more than livable wage, but they rejected me. After visiting an East Coast congregation, we decided to pass because the fit just did not seem right.

Eventually opportunities were narrowed to congregations in Fort Wayne and Bedford Indiana. After much prayerful wrestling, we decided on Bedford. It seemed the better fit. The church matched the vast majority of our criteria. The congregation needed healing in the aftermath of a serious conflict with the previous pastor. That seemed an interesting challenge. In addition to a better salary, the church offered to loan us the down payment for our first home. Although hesitant to credit Providence for what may have been only a human decision rooted in more money and better weather, this felt like a call from God.

The week after Thanksgiving we moved into a nearly new house about five miles from the church. We thought ourselves proud first-time homeowners. In reality, we were proud first-time mortgage holders. The bank and First Christian Church jointly owned the house. We began to pay $440 per month for insurance, real estate taxes and debt retirement. Thirty-five years and three mortgages later, we have yet to become paid-in-full homeowners.

As soon as possible we enrolled Karen and Colleen at Shawswick School. We were not impressed. The school was built in the early 1900s and appeared not to have been updated since. The building could have been modeled after the prison in the movie *Shawshank Redemption.*

We would learn the quality of the education matched the school's architecture. At the first parent conference, Karen's very caring teacher lamented that our eldest had already completed the work planned for that school year. It was only November. The teacher promised she would supplement Karen's instruction with individualized reading assignments to keep her occupied. Colleen's classroom was in the corner of a room formerly used to store coal. While not impressed by the building, we were appalled by the quality of the education. This proved to be a serious, ongoing, irresolvable issue.

Challenged as the Pastor

The Bedford congregation was a larger, more complex institution that pushed me on a multitude of fronts to learn and grow as a pastor and leader. I had to learn the proactive, managerial side of pastoral ministry. In Bedford I was introduced to congregational planning, working with committees, preparing an annual budget, funding the church's ministry with an annual fund drive as well as a host of other administrative tasks. Although neither as exciting as the adventure I fantasized on long winter days in Petoskey nor as spiritually uplifting as Moses' call to lead God's people out of Egypt, it was needed professional skill development.

Bedford, Indiana

The pastoral work began very well. We planned get-acquainted meetings at the church with the physically able and emotionally willing as well as home visits with shut-ins. The goal was to meet the people, hear their dreams for the church and, in the belief that it would be a healing balm, give congregants the opportunity to express their thoughts and feelings about the recent conflict over the previous minister. Although the meetings did not elicit many dreams, I learned a great deal about the membership. Unfortunately, these gatherings also tapped a bottomless well of angry complaining.

Contrary to what some assert, encouraging people to express negative feelings is not necessarily healing or helpful. Rather than reducing vitriol, many folks find that talking about what irritates them feeds their anger. Frankly it is not necessary to encourage most people to express their negative feelings. It comes naturally.

The issue that generated the most negative comment was an administrative reorganization of the Christian Church (Disciples of Christ) called Restructure. To oversimplify a very complicated issue, this was a carefully planned, extensively vetted effort to bring some meaningful order to the denomination's plethora of loosely connected agencies, committees and societies. Although the Restructure process had received some negative comment nationally, it had degenerated in Bedford to a nasty fight between those who considered themselves Cooperative with the Disciples and those who considered themselves Independent of the Disciples.

The disagreement had been festering since 1910 when Sam Lappin, an early leader of the Independent Movement, became pastor of the Bedford congregation. Restructure discussions lit a fuse on this issue that exploded in a series of angry, name-calling congregational meetings. Eventually the Independents, about 40 percent of the membership, left to form a new congregation on the other side of town.

When I arrived a decade later, the ill will over Restructure and the ensuing church split was still a raw, open wound. Although not all, certainly a large minority of the members brought up this topic in get-acquainted meetings. They spoke of the controversy as if it had happened the month before I arrived, not a decade before.

The combination of the Restructure controversy and the complaints about the previous minister led to too many conversations in which angry, red-faced parishioners with carotid arteries pulsating expressed themselves. I came to understand that this was not out of the ordinary behavior in Bedford. Nursing grudges and angry complaining were simply part of the community's cultural fabric.

One congregational leader and trusted friend described this as an extension of local history. "It all started before the Revolutionary War on the frontier of North Carolina," he told me. "There was a group of disagreeable settlers who just could not get along with their Carolina neighbors. Squire Boone, Daniel's father, led that group through the Cumberland Gap into the frontier of central Kentucky. After a few generations, the descendants of those Carolinians got to arguing with their Kentucky neighbors. The dispute became so heated they left and moved to Indiana. They were just as disgruntled in Bedford, but decided to stay. Their descendants have nearly perfected grumbling and complaining. That pattern has resulted in this small town having two hospitals, two Masonic Temples and too many churches. We get to fighting about one thing or another and the next thing you know, we split into two groups. We just do not play nicely with one another."

In another conversation with that same man, I mentioned my surprise at the longevity of Bedford residents. "We must have thirty members of the church who are over ninety," I said to him.

"Yep," he responded. "That is another part of our history. Most of us are descended from Scotch-Irish stock. For us, long life is common. In fact, when they founded this town, they had to shoot a guy just to get the cemetery started."

That fellow had a delightful way to tell local history. He was also enormously supportive and appreciative of the new minister, as were most of the church members.

Some contend it is easy to assess the state of a congregation. The people vote on it every Sunday. If they like what is happening, they come to church and open their checkbooks. If they don't like what is going on, they stay home and slap closed their checkbooks.

By that standard, things went very well in Bedford. Membership, attendance and income boomed. In addition, program life was expanded and deepened. It was easy to be very pleased with the Bedford ministry experience.

I felt particularly good about my preaching. From the beginning of my ministry, I made sermon preparation a priority. In Bedford, I began to make even more of an effort and the congregation was encouraging in their evaluation. Consequently, my preaching improved.

A Sampling of Things Ministers Do

The work of a local church pastor has incredible variety. Each week hours are devoted to sermon and worship preparation. In any particular seven-day period the minister might also marry a young couple so passionately in love their joy is infectious; catch a glimpse of the presence of God during a visit with a mother and her newborn child; explain to the committee planning the city's fourth of July celebration why the ministerial association objects to the parade being held on Sunday morning; be at the bedside of a parishioner at the moment of death; comfort that person's family; conduct the funeral; and still spend three days in court with a family while their son is being tried for illegal drug sales. Ministry can be stressful. More often it is meaningful, interesting and fulfilling.

I continued a ministry in pastoral counseling in Bedford and, for that matter, in every congregation I served. As with many congregational ministers, many of my most memorable experiences have come from more than three decades of these private conversations with ordinary human beings about the most intimate details of their lives.

To illustrate, I offer a sampling of stories from different congregations and situations. Please note that names have been changed and locations omitted to protect confidentiality.

A Bride Who Did Not Understand Commitment

George and Marilyn were in their mid-20s. They met the previous year and were madly in love. They seemed very compatible. There were no red flags raised during the premarital conversations.

I recall Marilyn as a very beautiful bride. A week or two after the wedding, Linda and I went to the local movie theater and Marilyn was the model in a pre-movie advertisement. I pointed her out to Linda and she agreed, "That is one gorgeous woman." The only other detail about her I remember is that her wedding ring was significantly larger than the groom's. That struck me as odd because the husband was not a particularly small man and she was not a particularly large woman.

Six weeks after the wedding, George came to see me. He was terribly distraught. "We are divorcing," he said. "I came home from work and found her in our bed with another man. She met him at work after our honeymoon, liked him and invited him home. She doesn't even seem to understand why I am upset by her behavior!"

Facial beauty and finger size aside, Marilyn had failed to grasp the meaning of the commitment section of the wedding vows. Her fidelity to "in sickness and in health until death do us part" lasted a month and a half.

An Issue In County Government

Bill and Jeannette had gotten involved in a spouse-swapping relationship with three other couples. To save their marriage, they wanted out. There was, however, a complication. Jeannette's boss and his wife were also part of this group. The boss was an elected county official and had threatened to fire Jeannette if she and Bill reneged on this sordid compact.

Their involvement had begun the previous year when Jeannette's boss invited her to have an intimate relationship with him. Partly because it promised a little excitement in her otherwise boring routine and partly because she sensed a threat to her job if she rejected the boss's offer, Jeanette agreed. The two began regular intimate encounters. Most were in motel rooms, but on occasion, they used the floor behind the customer service counter when the office was closed for lunch. About two months into the affair, Jeanette learned the boss had a similar arrangement with two other married women in the same office.

Six months into the affair, the boss's wife discovered what had been going on. Rather than demanding an end to his exploits, she proposed an expansion on her husband's activities. If the husbands of his employees agreed to get involved, she would join the group and they could have Eight Person Spouse-Swapping Parties.

I am uncertain how eight people in four different marriages agreed to this. Maybe the women employees, concerned for their jobs, didn't see an alternative. Maybe the husbands thought this behavior was acceptable. Whatever the reasons, four couples became involved. Since the county office where the boss and three women employees worked was not large enough to accommodate their group, the Swap Parties occurred on weekend camping trips.

After Jeannette managed to transfer to another office in the County Building, she and Bill cut their ties with that set of tangled relationships. Eventually, they moved. I never heard what happened to the others in the group. I do, however, continue to feel uneasy when I have business to transact in government offices over a customer service counter.

Secrets That Should Not Have Been Kept

When he called he told me his name was Don and someone had given him my name. He needed help with a decision. When he arrived at the office, he handed me two envelopes. Both contained the results of a medical test—no sperm present.

"Those test results are mine," he said. "My daughter is sixteen. My wife had a terrible time delivering her. The doctor told me that there was a good chance she would die if she had another child. I didn't tell my wife what the doctor said. Instead, I got a vasectomy. I never told her about that either. Recently, I learned my wife is pregnant. To find out if the child is mine, I had those tests. Today the results came in the mail. They prove the vasectomy did not fail. I am sterile. Obviously my wife is having an affair with someone. I have a decision to make and I wanted to talk to you first. Do you think I should go home and throw all my wife's things in the front yard or should I go home and kill her?"

"Perhaps," I said, "you should consider other alternatives. The evidence seems to indicate your wife has had a relationship outside your marriage. Her unfaithfulness hurts. You have already said you believe that warrants ending your marriage. However, you have also deceived her. You never told your wife that another pregnancy would jeopardize her life as well as the life of the baby. You kept life and death information from her. Whether or not her pregnancy ends your marriage, doesn't she deserve to know what you know?"

Don reluctantly agreed. He went home and had what must have been a difficult conversation with his wife. The next day they both came to see me. Sarah, Don's wife, had had an affair with a neighbor who lived about a mile down the road, but it had ended. Both Don and Sarah agreed, however, that divorcing was a good decision. Their marriage had been seriously troubled for years. They had also decided that, given Don's secret information about Sarah's health problem, she would terminate the pregnancy.

Although both were opposed to abortion, Sarah's life was in jeopardy. Don was adamant that he did not want custody of their teenage daughter in the event of Sarah's death. In these circumstances, they had decided an abortion was the less objectionable option.

At the time, it was necessary for Sarah to go out of state for the procedure. Don funded the trip. As soon as possible, Don and Sarah divorced. Within a few months, he moved to a distant large city. Sarah stayed in town, continued at her job and raised their daughter. She never remarried.

Five years later, Don and Sarah's now grown daughter decided to marry. Because the family knew no other minister, the bride, groom and Sarah asked me to perform the ceremony. I agreed. Don, the bride's father, came to the wedding. By then, he was leading an openly gay life. In the five years since I met him, he had gone from being an angry, miserable person to a man at peace with himself.

One simply cannot predict the strange twists lives can take. After struggling with lies, deceit, unfaithfulness, and an incredibly difficult decision on a life and death matter, Don was a happy man. Sarah was a happy woman. Their daughter had grown into a fine young adult. I do not know if they all lived happily ever after, but at the wedding five years later, they were doing better than I would have ever predicted.

What Tangled Webs We Weave When First We Seek To Decieve

Although Jill and Betsy lived in the same mobile home park, they did not know each other. I seemed to be their only connection. Both were going through difficulty and sought me out for pastoral guidance and support.

Betsy was childless and about thirty years old. She had recently divorced, had no family or friends in the area and needed someone with whom to talk. Even though she was not a member of the church, she sought me out. Mostly she talked and I listened. Gradually the dark cloud over her life began to lift. After a several weeks, she came to an appointment with a smile on her face and a lilt in her step. She had met a man. His name was Luke and he worked as a state drug enforcement agent. Betsy chattered on and on about this wonderful fellow. I was happy for her, of course, but the more details she offered about Luke the more suspicious I became. Something was just not right. I did not share my reservations with Betsy. Instead, I told her I was happy for her, but "If you need me, you have my phone number."

Jill, about the same age as Betsy, was divorced with two small children. She had been living in California and recently had moved east to her hometown and the church where I was the minister. After her divorce, she met Nathan. They fell in love. Although they did not marry, they lived together. He had moved with Jill and her children from California.

Jill sought me out because she wanted to end her relationship with Nathan. He had become a financial and emotional burden. She was, however, reluctant to rid herself of him. She worried about Nathan's mental health. As she explained, Nathan had experienced more than his share of tragedy. He had once played football at the University of Nebraska and had been drafted as an offensive lineman by the Oakland Raiders. Prior to moving to California, his wife and infant son were killed in an automobile accident. In spite of crushing grief, he had moved to Oakland with hopes of starting a new life. Unfortunately, his professional football playing days ended prematurely with a serious knee injury. When the two met, as Jill put it, "Nathan was a basket case. I took him in and nursed him back to health. It was hard work. It took everything I had to offer. He seems fine now and I want to end our relationship. I fear, however, what a breakup will do to him."

After several conversations with Jill, I invited her to bring Nathan. Her live-in boyfriend looked the part of an NFL lineman. He was so tall and wide he had to bend down and turn sideways to get through the door into my office. As we talked, I began to notice that some of the details of Nathan's life did not fit reality. For instance, he placed the University of Nebraska in Omaha rather than Lincoln and credited his psychiatrist with saying and doing things that a professional would not say or do. I also noticed that when I pressed him on contradictions in his story, he would spin his explanation into something almost plausible. I came to realize that Nathan had a problem and I was out of my depth.

I referred Nathan and Jill to a local therapist. Part of that referral was to secure their consent for the therapist and me to share information that would otherwise be confidential. The signed document proved very helpful. In a matter of weeks, it became obvious that Nathan was, for lack of a better term, a pathological liar, a master of deceit and a specialist in taking advantage of naïve young women.

The lives of Jill and Betsy intersected when we discovered they were involved with the same man. Jill knew him as Nathan, a former professional football player who had lost his wife and child. Betsy knew him as Luke, an undercover drug agent. Nathan/Luke also had a different name and different identify at a part-time job in town. He never played football in the NFL. For that matter, he never attended a college. He was from California, not Nebraska. He never lost a wife and child in an auto accident because he never married and never had a child. When he met Jill, he was not twenty-six years old. He was nineteen. He never had been employed as a drug enforcement officer. He simply made up names and identities.

Both Jill and Betsy managed to end their relationships with him and send him on his way. About a year later, he married another young woman using a different name and identity. About that time, I relocated. Fifteen years later, I returned to visit the congregation. Jill was still an active member with nearly grown children. She never remarried and had no idea what happened to Nathan/Luke/Whoever.

Early in my career I wrote the following in a church newsletter article. It still summarizes how I feel about being the minister of a local congregation.

BEING A MINISTER MEANS…

…spending three years studying systematic theology only to discover the most scholarly comment people respond to is "God loves you."

…never having enough money to pay one's bills or enough time to count one's blessings.

…receiving two anonymous letters in the same week. One written to correct the grammar in last Sunday's sermon, the other containing money for a family in need.

…seldom living near relatives, but always near friends.

...trying not to laugh when asked to say a blessing of the town's new sewage treatment plant.

...always working overtime, but seldom feeling the need to watch the clock.

...uniting with God's children at all the turning points of life.

...sharing the joys at the wedding and the tears in the hospital and funeral home.

...pushing the button of hope for those whose life has hit bottom.

So Much Went Well and Yet

In addition to feeling blessed that we were able to purchase our first home, we established some wonderful friendships in Bedford. Lowell and Marion Davis served as loving, supportive substitute parents to Linda and me, as well as proxy grandparents to Karen and Colleen.

They were absolutely wonderful people.

George and Barbara Sorrells became good church friends. We have reconnected since our move to Lexington. Three or four times each year we meet for dinner and conversation in Louisville, halfway between Bedford and Lexington. Another three or four times each year, Linda and Barbara meet in Louisville for three to four hours of lunch, shopping and conversation.

While in Bedford, Bill and Carol Duncan offered what might be called a friendship of presence. Just being together was a joy. Our families spent many delightful days at summer picnics at Spring Mill State Park and winter dinners at one another's homes. As couples we also survived one of marriage's most stressful activities—canoeing. Few things test a relationship as much as a husband and wife negotiating an unstable boat on a fast-moving stream. I recall that as we were beaching canoes on the shore for the day's first rest stop, I inquired how things were going with them. Bill maintained a longstanding tradition of couple canoeing by blaming his wife. "After we capsized the third time, I told Carol 'We have been married twenty-one years and until today, I never thought of you as stupid.' Other than that, things are going pretty well," he said. Friends are one of life's great blessings.

We purchased a second car while in Bedford. We lived five miles from town and Linda needed a reliable way to get to stores, schools and appointments. A second car also set Linda free from some of her all-consuming duties as Home Office Manager and Child Care Specialist. For the first time since Karen was born, every once in a while Linda could do something she wanted to do, including working part-time at a fabric store and meeting friends for lunch. It was a grace-filled opportunity for her and thus a blessing for me and the girls.

How wonderful it was to watch our children's growth during the Bedford years. Colleen was in early elementary school. The delightful personality and bubbly presence she brings as an adult were beginning to evidence themselves. I loved watching her with her friends and her dog. She was a source of sheer joy. Karen was moving through late elementary and middle school and was starting to rise to the challenges of growing up. She continued the piano lessons she started in Petoskey and became quite good. She won the spelling bee at Shawswick School, but lost in the city-wide contest. I was pleased both that she experienced the joy of victory and learned the lessons only defeat can teach.

I have an especially fond memory of Karen and me camping in the rain with the church youth group on Lake Bloomington. How impressed I was by Karen's physical strength as well as her tenacity in dealing with the difficult weather. She endured without complaining, which is more than could be said for her father.

Of course, everything did not go perfectly in Bedford. Late one night, Linda discovered a breast lump. Although it took less than forty-eight hours for the doctor to diagnose and aspirate a benign cyst, it was the longest two days of my life. Never had I experienced worry of that magnitude. My stomach hurt. Anxiety wrapped its tentacles around my chest until I could hardly breathe. I could think of nothing else. When the doctor informed us there was nothing about which to worry, it seemed a thousand pound weight was lifted.

In addition to giving thanks to God for good news, I changed one of my pastoral practices. Previously, I encouraged parishioners awaiting medical test results not to worry. I learned from personal experience that was foolish advice. Waiting in the perilous unknown leads naturally to worry. It comes with being human. After this encounter with my own anxiety, I began to pray with parishioners, "Lord, these people are understandably worried. They do not know what is going to happen with these tests. Grant them the power of Your Holy Presence that they might be kept from being overwhelmed by worry and uncertainty." In a curious way, I think I was a more effective pastor because of a benign cyst.

As noted, we had a bad first impression of Bedford public schools. Unfortunately, nothing changed. Our girls were just not going to get an excellent education in this school system. As parents we had to do better by our children, even if it meant moving.

How We Came to Move to Bloomington

Early in my third year at Bedford, I was invited to do a series of Lenten lectures at First Christian Church in Bloomington, Indiana, about twenty-five miles north of Bedford. Located near the campus of Indiana University, it was an impressive ecclesiastical institution. Frankly, I was flattered that they invited me and quickly accepted.

I enjoyed the people who came each week and thought I did a pretty good job in my presentations. Apparently they agreed because a couple of months later their senior minister resigned and their search committee asked me to be a candidate for the pulpit. Once again, I was flattered and quickly agreed. I may have even thought, "This must be a sign from God. Why else would they flatter me *twice?*"

Although this congregation had many strong applicants, I came to believe I was the most likely choice. Members of their search committee came to hear me preach no fewer than six Sunday mornings. My references called to say the committee had inquired about me. I was confident. They were going to choose me. Surely, God is in the midst of this.

How shocked I was to learn John Trefzger, a minister twenty years my senior, had been called. How could that search committee have failed to understand that God wanted me at their church? I was devastated.

After John settled into First Christian Church, Bloomington, Indiana, we had a get-acquainted lunch. I mentioned that I was one of the candidates for his new job. He said, "My son is on the search committee at the other Bloomington, First Christian Church—the one in Illinois. If you are interested, I can tell him about you."

I said, "Sure, go ahead." John called his son. A few months later we were on the way to the other Bloomington, First Christian Church.

There are some peculiarities about that move that make me believe Bloomington, Illinois really was a call from God. (1) I did not get a raise by leaving Bedford. (2) The interest rate on the Bedford mortgage was 6 percent. It was 14 percent on the Bloomington mortgage. (3) Our mortgage payment doubled and our real estate taxes tripled. (4) It was nearly a year before we sold our Bedford home. In the meantime, we paid 21 percent on our equity swing loan.

Those seem clear indicators of God's call to me. Perhaps that was part of why our time in Bloomington was my most fulfilling in ministry as well as a wonderful time for our family.

6

Glorious Salad Days
on the Prairie

In spring 1980, I went to a church growth conference in Amarillo, Texas. One of the speakers commented, "Sometimes the best thing you can say about where you are in life is that it is on the way to something else." That resonated. In spite of multiple reasons to rejoice, serving the Bedford congregation was more burdensome than rewarding. That is understandable. Leadership among people who claim not to play well together will be more difficult. It was helpful to think of Bedford as on the way to something else.

Of course, I did not know at the time this new destination would be my ministry's *Salad Days.* By that I mean my most fulfilling service to Christ and the Church. When I went there, I was thirty-eight years old. My energy and skill level was beginning to peak. The near decade we spent in Bloomington was a ministry highlight.

Of course, every circumstance was not perfect. The national economy was wretched. Home mortgage interest rates were historically high and, for a full year, we were unable to sell our home in Bedford. That meant we had two house payments plus the interim loan on the Bedford equity. To meet this financial burden, Linda went to work fulltime. After years of being our stay-at-home Mom and Cueni Clan Home Office Manager, this was a significant family change. Fortunately, Linda made it work for the benefit of all.

Upon arrival, we enrolled Karen and Colleen in school. Karen went to ninth grade at the junior high two blocks from our home. Colleen went to sixth grade at a more distant elementary school. Our children's first weeks at their new schools were the opposite of what had happened at Shawswick. Normal Community schools offered an excellent education.

Two Quick Stories about This Author and His Daughters

Karen and Colleen were understandably reluctant to leave friends and familiar surroundings simply because Dad decided to move the family. Therefore, I promised that even if I had to leave ministry and sell used cars, they would graduate from high school before the family relocated again.

On the drive between Indiana and Illinois, Karen grumbled, "I will make this move, but when I graduate from high school, I am going to move back to Bedford and spend the rest of my life there."

When high school graduation neared and people asked me where Karen was going to college, I told them, "She wants to go the University of Mars, the farthest place from home she can find." She graduated from Texas Christian University, about 900 miles from Bedford. After college she taught in Kenya, East Africa, and later in Belize, Central America. Eventually she settled near Houston, Texas, physically a 1000 miles and culturally light years from Bedford, Indiana. Obviously, she changed her mind about living her life in southern Indiana.

One warm spring afternoon, Colleen's sixth grade attention span surpassed its outer limit. She was daydreaming. Her teacher, Mr. Schweers, called on her to answer a question. Rather than admit her inattentiveness, she blurted the first thing that popped into her mind, "Florida!" Her teacher made that Colleen's nickname. More than thirty years later, Mr. Schweers still addresses Colleen as "Florida" in their Facebook communications.

Fortunately, we lived in Bloomington until both girls left home. I did not have to make good on my promise to leave the ministry. I would have been terrible at used car sales.

Bloomington, Illinois

A Historic City and Church on the Prairie

In 1980, Bloomington was a city of 40,000 with a metropolitan population a little less than 100,000. It is situated on the prairie halfway between Chicago and St. Louis on some of the nation's richest farmland. The topsoil is as black as potting soil and is said to be sixty feet deep. The city was founded in the first third of the nineteenth century as a railroad center. The remnants of the old switching yards and repair shops still function, albeit with a greatly reduced workforce. Although growing corn and soybeans has become the most visible industry, the corporate headquarters for State Farm Insurance, Eureka Vacuum sweepers, Beer Nuts and Beich's Candy are also located there. Two universities, Illinois State and Illinois Wesleyan, anchor different ends of the same street. It all makes for a wonderfully diverse economy, not to mention a population that reflects the very best of Midwest American values.

Although Abraham Lincoln lived in Springfield before he became President, he had a significant presence in Bloomington. His law practice regularly brought him to town. The nation began to notice him after a speech in Bloomington during the founding convention of the Illinois Republican Party. Lincoln was first encouraged to run for the Presidency by the editor of the Bloomington Daily *Pantagraph*. As President, he named Bloomington lawyer, David Davis, to the U.S. Supreme Court. Bloomington is Lincoln Country.

The history of First Christian Church is equally interesting. The founding pastor, William Major, was a convert to the abolitionist cause. He moved from Kentucky to Illinois in 1837 after freeing his slaves. He became a friend of Lincoln and actually owned the Convention Center where the Illinois Republican Party was founded. Mr. Major was also a friend of Alexander Campbell, a founder of the Christian Church (Disciples of Christ). Campbell visited the church from time to time and actually owned land less than a mile from our house.

The most well-known pastor in the congregation's history was Edgar DeWitt Jones. He was in Bloomington from 1906-1916. After going to Detroit's Central Woodward Christian Church, he became one of the nation's most recognized preachers in the first half of the twentieth century.

When the congregation built a sanctuary in 1960, they dedicated the new pulpit in honor of Edgar DeWitt Jones. The first day I stood in that pulpit and saw the inscribed brass marker, I felt both proud and intimidated to stand in line behind this great preacher.

The pulpit from which Jones preached in the 1890 building was eventually moved to a Sunday School classroom. It has a brass plate listing all the ministers who had preached from that pulpit. John Trefzger, the former minister whose son was on the search committee that called me, said he was responsible for that plaque. "I bought and installed it because I knew it was the only way my name would appear on a list with Edgar DeWitt Jones."

Life as Pastor of this Congregation

The congregation had a long history of loving their ministers and grieving their departures. Roger and Mary Zimmerman, the husband and wife team who preceded me, fit that pattern. People loved the Zimmermans. They valued Mary's excellent educational programming and Roger's highly intentional pastoral care. The congregation's grief at their departure for Corvallis, Oregon, was still palpable when I arrived. In fact, one woman told me, "You will never replace Roger as my pastor." Others initially felt the same way. Fortunately, it was only a matter of a few months before the love and appreciation felt for the Zimmermans was transferred to the Cuenis.

That does not mean, of course, there was never a stressful encounter or discouraging word. On my second Sunday I was in the narthex waiting for the organ prelude to conclude and the first hymn to begin. The choir, also waiting in the narthex, had yet to stop chattering and fall in line for the processional. No one told me Roger Zimmerman lined up the choir and quieted their conversations. Burt Mercier, a member of the choir, apparently believed hushing and organizing choirs was high on the list of Pastoral Best Practices. Burt, who never had an unexpressed opinion, came up to me, placed a finger in my chest and said, "Cueni, you are not demonstrating enough leadership to organize a two-car funeral. Do something about this choir."

Burt made this comment with his usual louder-than-necessary voice. At first, I was offended. As I gathered my thoughts for how to respond without escalating the conversation into a shouting match, I noticed a tiny smile appear at the corners of his lips. Burt intended to be clever, not accusatory. I laughed, quieted the choir and organized them for the processional. That became an every Sunday procedure.

The first week of December in my first year, I received a letter from the Bloomington Fire Chief saying that "because of the fire hazard posed by individuals lighting candles on Christmas Eve, the practice had been banned by city ordinance."

The letter was shared with the chairperson of the worship committee. Like me, she was relatively new to the city and the church. We agreed the law had to be obeyed. It was mentioned in the next week's newsletter that the congregation would be using small flashlights instead of candles at the Christmas Eve service.

That announcement divided the congregation. On one side were those who insisted, "It is the law and we must follow it." On the other side were those who argued that tradition dictated lighted candles on Christmas Eve. "Neither the City Council nor the Fire Chief can tell us what to do. We are adults."

The debated raged for about a week when Burt Mercier came to see me. Several weeks previously, he had raised questions about my leadership ability in quieting and organizing the choir. Instead of the anticipated repeat of that type of discussion, he offered a helpful perspective. "Bob," he explained, "that is not a <u>new</u> city ordinance. The Fire Chief sends that letter every year and every church in town ignores it. Trust me, the precautions we have in place are sufficient. Now, I suggest you let the congregation know we are going to continue the meaningful tradition of lighting candles on Christmas Eve. If you do that, much of the current stress in your life will disappear."

From these exchanges with Burt, several valuable lessons were learned. (1) Every church has well-established, but unwritten and unspoken traditions. The new minister will often be introduced to them in unconventional or even pain-filled ways. (2) Unless there are compelling reasons to discontinue a meaningful tradition, maintain it. Wise is the minister who remembers it is easier to ride a horse in the direction the horse is already going. (3) Politicians take heat from changing their minds. In the political arena this is called flip-flopping and is to be avoided. In ministry, changing one's mind is not only acceptable, it may indicate pastoral wisdom. (4) Try not to wear your feelings on your sleeve. It makes life simpler and easier.

Between the second and third years in Bloomington, I invited Herb Miller, the Executive Director of the Disciples' National Evangelistic Association and a respected church consultant, to come to Bloomington to do a Parish Enrichment Conference. I thought the church could benefit from what Herb had to offer. Congregational leadership agreed.

The Parish Enrichment Conference began with several weeks of preparation by church members and leaders. Small groups met to discuss issues. Surveys were given. Statistical reports were compiled. The pile of information we sent to Herb was nearly three inches thick. By the time he arrived, he knew a great deal about First Christian Church.

The event was a mixture of one-on-one meetings with Herb, all-church fellowship dinners, skill-building workshops and an old-fashioned revival meeting. A sense of commitment and enthusiasm began to infect the congregation. Only the most peripheral members were untouched by the Parish Enrichment Conference.

At its conclusion, Herb mailed us fifty copies of a 100-page book of information and analysis with ninety-one suggestions of things we could do to enrich the life of the congregation. The suggestions applied to each of the committees, e.g., worship, evangelism, property, pastoral care, Christian Education, outreach, personnel, etc. That book and those suggestions became the equivalent of our Long Range Plan. For the next few years, each committee annually picked a few of the suggestions and implemented them.

By the time Bloomington, First had exhausted the programmatic possibilities suggested in our Parish Enrichment Conference book, the congregation was much more effective at its mission and ministry.

That booklet was the first *implemented* multi-year plan the church had. One had been *developed* a few years previously. However, at its completion, the notebooks were placed on a library shelf. If asked, leaders were able to say, "Yes, we have a plan." It found no other use. The Parish Enrichment Conference had produced a simple, workable plan that made a difference. From that I learned a valuable lesson: It is not enough to plan your work. You have to work your plan.

During the same time frame another evangelism and church growth conference was announced for Louisville, Kentucky. I had found the one in Amarillo meaningful and encouraged several Bloomington lay leaders to attend. Not only did the group return filled with enthusiasm, the lay leadership caught a vision for church growth from that conference. The following year nearly one hundred people joined First Christian Church. This taught me another valuable lesson. Involving a congregation's lay leadership produces better results than simply having the minister involved.

The congregation's 150th anniversary and a $1.2 million Capital Campaign were two other events during our Bloomington decade around which significant programming was planned. The church's birthday observance was more fun than work. The Capital Campaign and subsequent construction were more work than fun.

Bloomington First Christian was founded in 1837, not long after the city's founding. In fact, the congregation claims to be the town's oldest continuing faith community. We planned a year-long celebration for the Sesquicentennial in 1987. Among other things, we updated the history, published a cookbook and celebrated an "Old Fashioned Sunday." At worship that day, congregants were encouraged to dress as though it was an earlier era. The prelude, hymns and postlude were chosen from early nineteenth century American composers and were played on a century-year-old pump organ. I led worship in a Prince Albert cutaway tuxedo, attire common for Disciple ministers from the middle of the nineteenth century until the late 1940s. I also found and preached an Edgar DeWitt Jones sermon he had delivered at Bloomington, First in 1912.

The church had not had a Capital Campaign since the new sanctuary was built nearly a generation previously. One was long overdue. We raised sufficient pledges to remodel much of the interior of the building by adding gathering space outside the sanctuary, expanding the offices, and adding an elevator, additional Sunday School classrooms, a new church parlor and a Schantz Pipe Organ.

The Sesquicentennial celebrations as well as the fundraising and renovations were marvelous experiences. It was a great time to be the minister of the church.

Personal Study and Development in Bloomington

While still in seminary I decided to become a lifelong learner. I was faithful to that commitment in my working years and continued to read and study in my retirement. Thanks to a natural intellectual curiosity, lifelong learning has been relatively easy. In fact, it has been and remains a source of enormous satisfaction. In Bloomington I added a different kind of learning to my usual habits of regularly attending educational events and reading on a wide variety of subjects. I discovered the educational value of travel.

During my third year in Bloomington, Herb Knudsen, a minister colleague in the Chicago area, alerted me to an inexpensive 10-day tour to Israel and Egypt. He was going and urged me to attend. At first I was reluctant. For years, I had made jokes about ministers taking trips to the Holy Land so they can claim to have walked where Jesus walked.

Herb Knudsen, however, was persistent and persuasive. He convinced me to accompany him. We juggled and stretched the household budget. I returned from the trip thankful for a persistent and persuasive friend. It was an incredibly important learning experience. It changed many of my understandings of the Bible and enriched my preaching.

A trip to Kenya, East Africa, a few years later was equally enriching. Not only did I get to visit Karen who was teaching in a small village in the western part of the country, I encountered lifestyles that differed greatly from those on the Illinois Prairie.

I have also been blessed by trips to Scotland, England, Ireland, Wales, Germany, Denmark, Austria, France, Belgium, Switzerland, Belize, Mexico, Costa Rica and a few others. There is truth in the wall poster saying, "When you are stretched over a new experience, you never shrink back to the same size."

A Couple of Mysteries from My Writing Hobby

Through the years, I had continued to write and submit sermons and magazine articles for publication. While in Bloomington, I expanded my repertoire with a poem and a book. The poem was written for the church newsletter. It received favorable comment and was submitted to *The Disciple* magazine. They published it. By way of some mysterious process, the poem was reproduced in a number of other publications, including *The John Milton Magazine for the Blind.* Imagine that. My poem was translated into Braille.

Here is that unrhymed, free verse as it appeared in the church newsletter:

IT ALL DEPENDS
One atom of carbon has no real value.

Combined, they form dazzling diamonds or charcoal lumps.
It all depends on heat intensity.
People are the same. Alone: meaningless.
Combined, we form a friendly community or a ghetto of hate.
The choice is ours.
We can live as if life's a bit of coal.
Or let God's light purify and transform our barriers of fear into
diamonds.

Poetry, I have been told, is difficult to publish. When my very first poem made it into print, I decided to stop writing poetry. That makes it possible to claim, "I am one of the few poets in the English-speaking world with a 100 percent rate of publication."

About halfway through my tenure on the prairie, I developed an urge to write a book on pastoral ministry. Precisely why this seemed a good idea is even more mysterious than why anyone would publish or republish my doggerel.

The home computer was still a novelty, but we made the decision that one was necessary. We expended a sizeable percentage of the family savings, a little more than $1,200, to purchase a computer, a black and white monitor and a small printer. Instead of a hard drive, the computer used two six-inch floppy discs. One contained the word process operating system. The other saved what was being written.

The manuscript took about a year to complete. It might have been done in less time, but the computer had the annoying habit of periodically displaying the screen, "You have just made a fatal error." The monitor then went blank and the entire day's writing disappeared, never to found again. What constituted that fatal error is another unresolved mystery.

When completed the manuscript was sent to a trusted colleague for a critique. Based on his comments, it was rewritten and sent to a book publisher. Within a few weeks, it was rejected. In Petoskey, Harold Kohn had taught me to respond to a rejection with a rewrite and submission to different publisher. His advice was scrupulously followed. That manuscript was rejected and rewritten another nineteen times before Abingdon Press accepted it for publication. The book is entitled, *What the Minister Can't Learn in Seminary: A Survival Manual for the Parish Ministry.* I still think of it as one of my best writing efforts. The source of the tenacity to keep at it until the book was published is another of those Bloomington writing mysteries.

The Grief Common to this Phase of Life

Professionally, the decade in Bloomington was the Glorious Salad Days on the Prairie. Within our extended family, it was an era of dealing with the declining health and eventual death of parents.

It began with Henry Andresen, Linda's father. Hank had been slipping for three or four years. We first noticed his decline during one of his last visits to Bedford. Advancing heart disease was rendering him less mentally alert and physically robust. In the ensuing months and years, his decline escalated. Linda took frequent trips to Ohio to be with her father. It was difficult to see him struggle with life's ordinary tasks. He was a wonderful man. Hank died in spring 1981, ten days after his sixty-ninth birthday.

Several years previously, Hank had completed a newspaper form on "Instructions for My Funeral." It listed everything from insurance policy and cemetery deed locations to details of his wishes for the funeral itself—including dressing him in his favorite three-piece brown corduroy suit and burying him in a highly polished wood casket "like the one my brother had."

I was impressed by how helpful Hank's instructions were to the family. By taking the time to complete that form, Hank saved his wife and daughters hours agonizing over estate and funeral details. For the rest of my ministry, I encouraged people to prepare a similar list for their family. I even wrote an article about it in the church newsletter. Although people were generally appreciative, I received a negative phone call from a florist in town. He strenuously objected to my father-in-law requesting people not to send flowers.

Linda's mother's health had started to decline before Hank's passing and continued to deteriorate until she died in 1988. When I first met Juanita in the middle 1950s, she was a tour de force. Officially she was the Secretary to the Stow High School Principal, but that designation hardly covered her duties as office manager, keeper of all permanent records, gate-keeper at the principal's office door, treasurer for the school's fund raising events, scheduler of all students and classes, front line problem solver for frantic and bewildered teachers and unofficial mother confessor as well as amateur psychotherapist to a student body of 700 hormone raging adolescents. When Juanita was in her prime, she not only excelled at the job, she loved it. When death came to release her from the struggle that life had become, she rejoiced at her passing to Glory.

Leona Cueni, my stepmother, died in 1984. Diabetes had plagued her for more than two decades. During her last few years, open wounds on her feet healed very slowly, if at all. As a result, she was frequently hospitalized for this condition; one year for more than 200 days.

As her mother before, Leona struggled with dementia during her declining years. I do not know if she had Alzheimer's disease. That term was yet to be in common use. Lay people and even physicians were more likely to explain dementia as hardening of the arteries in the brain. Whatever the cognitive malady, Leona spent the last couple of years of her life bedridden and unaware of much of the reality around her.

My father was enormously attentive to his wife during those last months and years. He visited her daily in the hospital or nursing home. He spoon-fed her meals and sat for hours by her bed. His care for her was one of the more pleasant surprises of my life. This was not typical behavior for Richard.

After I left home to marry in 1962, Richard began a quarter-century downhill slide. His "romantic liaison" and "daily fifth of distilled spirits" patterns continued. His drinking led to periodic binges in which he disappeared from home for a week or two. Often he would not even know where he had been until his credit card statement arrived the next month.

Occasionally he would recall something about his adventures. Once he told me, "I remember there were three or four other people in the room. I held a full bottle of vodka to my lips. My plan was to drain it without stopping. It occurred to me that if I did, I would probably die. I don't remember what happened after that."

My brother Jonathan tells of being with Dad when he arrived home after a bender. "He was still hung over when the phone rang," Jon said. "Apparently it was the husband of a woman who had been with him. All I heard, of course, was Dad's side of the conversation. 'I don't know where she is' he said. 'She was with me in Pennsylvania and I lost her.'" When one cannot keep track the whereabouts of one's romantic drinking companions, one's life has, indeed, become chaotic.

Every now and then, an effort was made to bring his life under control. In his early forties, he began attending AA meetings. Unlike the experience of my mother who was also in the program, Richard did not gain much benefit from AA. Periodically, he would enter a 30-day detoxification program. This might be at the urging of the family, a judge's sentencing or even by his choosing. These programs would be temporarily helpful, but in a few months he would start to drink again.

There are, of course, a finite number of alcohol rehabilitation programs in Ohio and surrounding states. At one time or another, my father had been a patient in most, if not all, of them. In fact, finding one that would admit him as a patient eventually became problematic. It got to the point that when the family called to have him admitted, facility after facility refused because they had declared him *persona non grata*.

This stemmed from two of Richard's opposing characteristics. On the positive side, my father made friends easily—particularly women and young adults. He could be enormously charming. On the negative side, he was highly skilled at using his charm to manipulate others. When he was in rehabilitation, he formed friendships. When he was ready for his next alcohol sojourn, he would locate one of those friends and convince him or her to accompany him. Because Dad was a regular disruption to the recovery of others, alcohol rehabilitation programs banned him.

Eventually, Dad was physically unable to consume alcohol. A single ounce of distilled spirits would hospitalize him with painful pancreatitis. During an occasional sober moment, it was possible to have a serious, albeit brief, conversation with him. He once explained that he was never really committed to AA. "I rejected the basic principles of the program. I don't really believe in a Higher Power. I never thought of myself as an alcoholic or as a person with a problem over which I had no control. In fact, if my body would permit it, I'd start drinking again. I really miss it." He continued by explaining that he used his time in alcohol rehabilitation, not to stop drinking, but to get it under control so that he could start all over again.

Dad moved Marie, a romantic liaison and periodic drinking companion, into the family home during Leona's final months in the nursing home. Marie remained with Richard until his death in 1989 shortly before his seventy-first birthday. Not only was Marie at his funeral, so were an assortment of Dad's other women and disheveled drinking companions.

Of note, the most distinguished callers at his funeral visitation were African Americans. My father had many faults, but racism was not among them. Several years before his death he had booked an ocean cruise for members of the Masonic Order. Dad had not read the fine print. The cruise was for Black Masons. Dad so enjoyed the voyage, he became a regular on Black Mason cruises. Several came to pay their respects at his funeral. Their presence at his visitation was a highlight.

When Richard's Last Will and Testament was read, we were surprised. After Leona's death he had changed it. His sons received only a couple of small items each. The house, his money and most of the family personal items were left to Marie, his live-in girlfriend. Although my brother Jon managed to retrieve many family photos and personal papers, the legal effort to contest the document failed. Marie invited many of her relatives to live with her in the house. After a year or so, she sold the house and kept the proceeds.

A Theological Dilemma

At the time of my father's death, the General Assembly of the Christian Church (Disciples of Christ) was debating a resolution on whether or not faith in Jesus Christ offers the only path to salvation. That resolution created a serious theological dilemma for me.

My father showed no particular interest in religious belief or practice. He had not gone to church regularly since he had been married to my mother. He was a totally undisciplined alcoholic. He was unfaithful to each of his wives. He claimed not to believe in a generic Higher Power. There was no deathbed confession, repentance or conversion. In fact, during one of his last hospital stays, he joked that he had been visited by the Catholic chaplain, a Protestant minister and a Jewish rabbi. To cover his bases, he claimed to be searching the phone book for Witch Doctors and Buddhist monks.

In spite of all his frailties, I loved my father, in part because I understood some of his journey. He was handed some difficult circumstances. In the terminology of the early twentieth century, his parents had to get married. Grandma was pregnant with Paul, my father's older brother who died of meningitis at the age of six. When I was child, Grandma Cueni was still reciting idealized memories of what she considered this nearly perfect little red-haired boy. My father was born about a year after Paul's death. Richard, I have concluded, felt that he could never compete with Paul's memory for his parents' attention and approval. From the stories I have heard about his childhood and adolescent school behavior, my father pretty much gave up seeking anyone's approval and began to act out in order to get attention. In a way, he never outgrew that.

Richard was also chronically depressed. Today depression is recognized as a serious, biochemical disorder requiring a specific medical response. That was not necessarily understood when Richard was a young adult. His physician prescribed tranquilizers for his anxiety and pain medication for his surgically repaired back. When the tranquilizers failed to lift his depression and the pain medication didn't control his back pain, Richard found additional physicians to prescribe more tranquilizers and painkillers. At the same time, he substantially increased his alcohol consumption. By his early forties he was regularly hospitalized for his addictions to tranquilizers and pain medications. He got these under control by his late forties. Unfortunately, his underlying depression was not diagnosed and treated until late in his life. By then, alcohol, his preferred self-treatment, controlled his life.

These observations are not intended to excuse my father's behavior. They do, however, help me understand what led to his becoming an unrepentant philanderer and uncontrolled drunk. As odd as it might seem, understanding him led me to accept him. Accepting him led me to love him.

The aforementioned General Assembly resolution said (To paraphrase): Therefore let it be resolved that those members of the Christian Church (Disciples of Christ) meeting in General Assembly affirm their belief that the only way to salvation is through faith in Jesus Christ.

On the one hand, this is a reasonably clear teaching of Scripture. In an otherwise uncomplicated world, I should agree and vote in the affirmative. Doing so, however, would mean that I would have to conclude my father died outside of God's love and grace.

I found that conclusion enormously troubling. The teaching of our faith is not necessarily uncomplicated. In addition to declaring, "No one can come to the Father except by me," the Scripture also contends that to love is to know God for God is love.

As disappointing and even as hurtful as was his behavior, I never gave up on my father or abandoned him to his plight. I simply could not imagine that God did. I loved and forgave my father. If God did not, my capacity for love and forgiveness would be greater than God's. I could not live with that conclusion. By definition, my love could not be greater than God's.

In some way more profound than my tiny mind can comprehend, let alone explain, God must have understood, loved, forgiven and welcomed my father into His presence—even if he did not affirm his faith and trust in Jesus Christ as Savior.

Dawn Strizak, my beloved mother, died in the late spring of 1999. She was about a month short of her seventy-seventh birthday. It had been a decade since the last death of a parent.

Heart disease was common in Mom's family. Whatever genes govern clogged arteries around the heart came to Mom with a vengeance. Over a period of a couple decades, she had major heart procedures on four different occasions, two open chest by-pass surgeries and two heart stent implantations.

The day before Mom's death, she and my sister Donna had been shopping. They had had a wonderful time. A photograph taken of her that day shows her seated in a favorite chair with a grin on her face. Donna's visit from California was a highlight of Mom's year.

The next morning, my mother was dressing for a routine physician's appointment. She sat on her bed to pull on her shoes. She gasped, fell backwards and died. Even as I grieved her death, I am comforted by that photograph. It is reassuring to know that the last full day of her life she had an ear-to-ear smile.

I talked with my mother every week. That regular communication is still missed. One of the last topics we discussed was the fact that Linda and I were about to become grandparents of twin girls. In part because she was a twin, Mom delighted in the idea of having twin great-grand- daughters. Unfortunately, Mom did not live to meet Elizabeth and Annika.

Mom Enjoying Donna's Visit

One day I was babysitting the twins. Still tiny, they were taking a nap in a living room bassinet. I was looking at them and thinking about how much my mother would have enjoyed these little girls. With my eyes fogged by the mist of loss, I turned my head toward the front window and caught a glimpse of my mother sitting on the living room sofa with an enormous smile on her face. I looked back at the sleeping twins and then turned again toward the sofa. Mom was not there.

I will not attempt to explain or to explain away that experience. I can say, however, it was reassuring and comforting. It reminds me of the promise of Jesus in the Gospel of Matthew assuring us He is with us always.

Grief at the death of my mother overwhelmed her husband, my stepfather, John Strizak. For the rest of his life, this proud, strong man was reduced to shoulder-shaking sobbing each time he spoke of Dawn Delores, his wife. He died two years later. His funeral was the same week as the 9-11 terrorist attacks. We had to drive from Kansas City to Akron because every airport in the United States was closed. Although we never had a close father-son relationship, when asked, I did not hesitate to conduct his funeral and deliver his eulogy. In spite of being an angry, controlling, verbally abusive, obsessive-compulsive patriarch, John Strizak had some fine qualities and he taught me some valuable lessons.

In evaluating my comments on the lives of my parents, especially my father and step-father, some will conclude I look through rose-colored glasses. Perhaps that is the case, but I really believe that difficult emotions like pain, suffering and disappointment play an important role in learning and growing. As a minister of the Church of Christ, I know that at the very heart of the Gospel is the cross, a symbol of the suffering and death that leads to resurrection and new life.

Hundreds of years before Jesus, the Greek poet and playwright, Aeschylus (b. 525 B.C.) expressed this truth from a different perspective: "*He who learns must suffer. And, even in our sleep, pain that cannot forget falls drop by drop on the heart; and in our own despair, against our will, wisdom comes to us by the grace of God.*"

7

The Road from Bloomington to Fort Worth to Kansas City

From idea to planning to fundraising to groundbreaking to construction to punch list, the capital campaign at Bloomington's First Christian Church took three years. The campaign grand finale was a Sunday evening dedicatory recital on the new pipe organ. The next morning, I arrived in the office an hour before anyone else. I needed the quiet time to meditate on the three discordant realizations:

(1) I had a sense of fulfillment. This faith community had pulled together for the campaign. It felt good to be their minister. In our years together, I had grown as a pastor and leader. The church had grown in their ministry and mission. As pastor and congregation, we had a wonderful relationship.

(2) I had accomplished my list of goals and objectives. We had responded to all the suggestions in the Parish Enrichment program, celebrated the 150th anniversary, completed the renovation and dedicated the pipe organ. The church needed a fresh long-range plan, and I needed to start doing the ground work for it.

(3) I was emotionally, spiritually and physically exhausted. The last three years had taken a toll. My energy needed to be replenished.

Given these circumstances, it might have been best to take an extended vacation for rest and renewal. If I had, it could have re-energized me and led to staying another ten years in Bloomington, Illinois. That congregation and I had a special relationship. For a variety of self-convincing reasons I began to entertain thoughts of making a career move. "My work here is finished." "It would be good to have more time to write." "Karen and Colleen are out of the nest and a change for Linda and me would be good."

No special action was taken. It was just a thought until I heard about an opening in Fort Worth for a new Trinity Brazos Area minister. A few inquiries were made. The next thing I knew I was headed for an interview at Dallas-Fort Worth Airport.

The position didn't seem particularly interesting. They wanted someone to be the pastor to pastors and representative of the mission and ministry of the Southwest Region for fifty-five Disciple congregations with 18,000 members in and around Fort Worth. To become an Area Minister meant giving up pastoral ministry for administration. Additionally, the interview did not go well. There was no meaningful chemistry with the committee. Only the fact that Karen and Colleen were living in Fort Worth made it appealing. I returned to Bloomington thinking we would not be going to Texas.

Imagine my surprise when the committee called a couple of days later and offered me the job. I told them that I would consider their offer. The next few days were filled with intense discussion with Linda, Karen, Colleen and ministry colleagues.

Herb Miller, our consultant on the Parish Enrichment program, had been a Texas Area minister. He highly recommended it. "It is a ministry," he said, "where your experience as a pastor will help other pastors and congregations. It is not a demanding or time-consuming job. The greatest thing about being an Area Minister is that, unlike pastoral ministry, you actually have time to do some of the things that you want to do. For instance, you can write books and do congregational consultations across the country."

The more Herb talked, the more appealing the job became. The family agreed and a positive answer was relayed to the search committee. Linda and I sold one house and bought another a thousand miles away.

The job as Trinity-Brazos Area (TBA) Minister had many benefits. Fort Worth is a lovely city with an outstanding Mexican restaurant on nearly every corner. Our home in the southwest corner of the city was beautiful. It was wonderful to have our young adult daughters living near-by. Texas Christian University, our church's largest institution of higher education, and its Brite Divinity School were within walking distance of the office.

The least positive aspect of living in Fort Worth was the office building. The Trinity Bazos Area minister had two cramped rooms on the second floor of a run-down house owned by the Southwest Region of the Christian Church. The carpet was worn, torn and appeared not to have been cleaned during its lifespan. The walls had not been painted for thirty or forty years. It was downright shabby. No wonder the search committee interviewed candidates at the Dallas-Fort Worth Airport. Within a few months, this new TBA minister moved the area office to an upper floor of the education wing at University Christian Church near the TCU campus. The work environment vastly improved.

A Note on my TBA Predecessor

Bert Cartwright was the previous TBA Area minister. In 1957 he was pastor of a small congregation in Little Rock, Arkansas. That year a Federal Court ordered the city's Central High School to racially integrate. As a teenager, I remember reading LIFE magazine reports of thousands of angry white citizens lining the streets to scream profanities and racial epithets at a handful of black children as they walked quietly into the formerly all-white school.

The story had circulated for years that Bert Cartwright had visited in the homes of each those black teenagers to encourage them and to explain that contrary to the protesters' behavior, not all white Christians hated them or opposed integrating the school system. In Little Rock in 1957, a white person offering kindness to black families was almost as controversial as the integration order itself. Bert might well have been fired by his church or received a late night visit from the Ku Klux Klan.

In 2011, more than a half century after the event, a national bestseller told the life story of one of the black high school students who walked through that angry mob. She named Bert Cartwright as one of the only white people in Little Rock who reached out to her and her family.

Throughout my ministry, Bert was considered a hero. I felt honored just to have known him.

Bert retired from the TBA a few weeks before my arrival. As he came to the end of his distinguished career, he built a file of the issues with which his replacement would need to deal. This three-inch thick stack of paper contained everything from letters that needed answering to memoranda on congregations currently searching for a minister to copies of heated correspondence with another area minister with whom Bert had differed on some matter.

In addition to dealing with the contents of that file, I immediately began to get acquainted with the ministers and congregations of the TBA. Within three weeks I was feeling so comfortable in the new job I returned to a project started in Bloomington—working on the manuscript for *The Effective Church Leader.* This was to be my second book with Abingdon Press. It differed from the first book in that Abingdon Press had agreed to publish it before it was written rather than after a plethora of rejections and rewrites.

It was not long before I drifted from being comfortable to being bored. There was just not enough to keep me busy. Linda recalls an evening early in our Fort Worth sojourn when I came home to tell her, "Linda I think WE have made a mistake." I responded to her query about "What do you mean WE?" with the admission I was using the editorial WE. "I have made a mistake. This is a miserable way to do ministry."

Eventually, I accepted reality. This job was not going to keep me as busy as I liked to be. I began to take a day off. Sometimes I even took a weekend off. I started doing consultations on behalf of Herb Miller and the National Evangelistic Association. I traveled to Philadelphia, Pennsylvania, Orlando, Florida, and Grand Forks, Nebraska for workshops with ministers on issues in church administration as well as to California's San Fernando Valley and Los Angeles to do congregational consultations on evangelism and church growth. Although I never particularly liked the travel, I enjoyed working with congregations and ministers.

The second year in Fort Worth, Dean Leo Perdue asked me to teach the church administration courses at Brite Divinity School while the faculty searched for a new professor in that position. I genuinely loved this opportunity to work with students.

In all honesty, I found little satisfaction as an area minister. The discontent was not, however, with what I was doing. It was with what I was not doing. I missed being the minister of a local congregation. Contrary to my thinking at the end of nearly a decade in Bloomington, I was not ready to go into some other form of ministry. I still wanted to lead a congregation.

Almost simultaneous to this realization, Gene Brice, Senior Minister at Country Club Christian Church in Kansas City, accepted a call to be Senior Minister at University Christian Church in Fort Worth. Gene's move awakened a fantasy of mine. From the time I graduated from Christian Theological Seminary, my career goal was to serve the largest congregation that would have me as its minister. Ecclesiastical upward mobility appealed to me.

Unfortunately, it is not proper for a minister to admit to wanting to be maximally challenged and paid a more comfortable living. That is considered unseemly for a servant of Christ. Therefore, when asked about career goals, I responded, "I want to be the Senior Minister of Country Club Christian Church in Kansas City, Missouri." For many years, I knew nothing about the congregation except that it had a funny name and was one of the larger faith communities in the Christian Church (Disciples of Christ). When I claimed a desire to go there, it sounded so preposterous my questioner usually had a good laugh and the conversation turned to other topics.

When Gene Brice went to University Church from Country Club, I asked the Regional Minister in Greater Kansas City to place my name into consideration. My joke about going to a *Country Club* Church was about to become a reality.

Area Ministry as Preparation for What Was to Come
The two year sojourn as an Area Minister was not my most satisfying. On the other hand, it was incredibly valuable. Without

the experience of working with a variety of pastors and congregations, each with a different approach to mission and ministry, the learning curves at both Country Club Christian Church and Lexington Theological Seminary would have been significantly steeper. Even though we can be bruised by life's bumps, the bumps can also polish us. It goes to show that "God is good. Indeed, God is good all the time."

The Challenge That Never Diminished

Country Club Christian Church was founded in 1920 in a planned residential area on Kansas City's growing far west side. Only a short walk from the Missouri/Kansas border, this neighborhood was the dream-in-progress of the developer, J.C. Nichols. His company had put in streets and city services, but as yet, there were few houses. The dominant institutions of the area were country clubs. Around the turn of the twentieth century, urban crowding had forced several to leave established neighborhoods and move to the otherwise undeveloped land on the far west side. Nichols appropriately named his new development The Country Club District. As the area grew, it acquired a reputation as the city's leading residential neighborhood. It maintained that status for decades. The local lore is that this beautiful city has more fountains than any city except Paris and more public statues than any city except Rome. Whether or not that it true, it is a wonderful place to live.

Originally named Country Club District Christian Church, the congregation grew as a reflection of the neighborhood's reputation. Within fifteen to twenty years of its founding in 1920, the congregation had 2,000 members, many of whom were among the city's social, political and business leaders. By 1950, the church grew to more than 3,000 members. By the 1990s, the church still had about 3,000 members, many of whom were business, social and political leaders.   In late winter 1990, the congregation began looking for its sixth senior minister in seventy years. Since this was not something they did often, it was assumed they would move slowly and be very thorough. Indeed, they were.

An Ill Wind

Every congregation's ministerial search committee pledges to work in secrecy. The rule is that if anyone tries to get inside information, tell them, "The search committee's proceedings are confidential." Unfortunately, the Disciples have a countervailing principle. In our church, confidentiality is defined as "Telling a secret to just one person at a time."

That countervailing principle was in play during the Country Club search. The committee might have thought they were doing their work in secret, but everything they did was more or less common knowledge on the Disciple Gossip Circuit. With one or two carefully placed phone calls, any candidate could get information about the search committee's inner workings. At one point, I heard from a half-dozen sources that a member of the Country Club Church was objecting to my being considered for senior minister.

I had once been on a personnel committee that dealt with the alleged inadequate job performance of a certain employee. The committee had recommended an early retirement. That person's daughter was a member of Country Club Church. Understandably, she was not pleased I was by being considered for the senior minister position.

The search committee took her concerns seriously. Committee members began gathering information, not only about that personnel committee decision, but on other aspects of me and my ministry. In doing so, the committee spent considerable time learning about my work in ministry; perhaps more than any other candidate. They must have been favorably impressed because they recommended me for the job.

In a curious way, the concerns of that early retiree's daughter may have been the deciding factor in my being called. As the aphorism goes, it is an ill wind that doesn't blow some good.

When the moving truck left Fort Worth for Kansas City, the driver informed us that we were his only stop and could expect delivery in two days. The two-day wait expanded to a full week. Somewhere between Texas and Missouri the driver found himself a woman. When the truck pulled into our Ward Parkway driveway, the driver's paramour was still with him. In fact, still wearing her full-length fur coat, this rather pleasant woman help unload the truck.

Our household goods arrived mid-morning on a Saturday. It was a long, tiring day of giving directives to the movers, arranging furniture, unpacking boxes and trying to maintain some semblance of order in the process. The next day was Sunday, always the busiest day of the week for a minister. I got up early that Lord's Day, dressed and headed off to church. I preached at the 9:00, 10:00, and 11:00 a.m. worship services. After the last service, a welcoming reception was held in Fellowship Hall. Following the shaking of several hundred hands, a few parishioners took us to lunch at one of the area country clubs. Without pausing for the traditional, divinely ordained Sunday afternoon nap, we worked late into the night unpacking boxes. Had it not been for Karen and Colleen coming to Kansas City to help, by Monday we might have collapsed into piles of exhausted dust.

The busyness of that weekend was to serve as boilerplate for life as the Senior Minister of Country Club Christian Church. I never worked longer, harder or smarter than in Kansas City. The demands of the job were unrelenting. This should not be understood as complaining. In fact, it was quite the opposite. I found deep satisfaction staying continually busy. For the first time in my ministry, I was never threatened by boredom.

The Christmas Eve service at Country Club Church was one of many wonderful traditions of this congregation. On my first December 24th I walked into a packed sanctuary for the 11:00 p.m. service. An additional hundred chairs were filled. The balcony was so crowded two people were sitting on top of the spare organ console and there were two rows of people standing against the back wall. More than 300 late arrivals had been turned away for lack of seating. The Kansas City Brass from the Symphony Orchestra was playing the prelude. I thought, "Wow! I am really going to like being the senior minister of this church."

Indeed, there was great satisfaction in this pastorate, although being minister at the 4Cs (shorthand for Country Club Christian Church) was not like other places. Rather than a pastor, I functioned as the congregation's Chief Executive Officer.

Actually that is not quite true. I was more the Chief Operating Officer, accountable to an entire congregation in which almost every member thought of himself or herself as the CEO. As we were fond of saying, the 4Cs had 3,000 Chiefs, but NO Indians. In spite of that challenge, or perhaps because of it, I believe my most effective work was in Kansas City.

In conversations with the search committee, I had learned staff morale was low. That was understandable. The senior minister of the previous thirteen years had left and the staff had been without a resident leader for a year. As the new senior minister I needed to make building staff morale my first priority. In reality, tending to staff cohesion occupied much of energy during my tenure. For the most part, I think I did a pretty good job. I had a wonderful time working with ministerial colleagues. The staff may or may not have felt the same way.

Improving office management was the primary agenda at an early planning retreat. The specific concern was to better coordinate the work of the ministers with the administrative staff. At the time, the ministry team consisted of six full-time ordained clergy: Senior Minister, Christian Education, Youth, Pastoral Care and Counseling, Singles/Young Adults and Church Growth. In addition, there was a licensed minister who served full-time as organist and choir director. He had a staff of three part-time musicians. The full-time administrative team consisted of business manager, bookkeeper, building manager, a custodian in residence and five secretaries. In addition, there was a half-time administrator for women's ministries. We had plenty of ministers and support staff but the ministry and mission of the 4Cs did not operate smoothly. At our retreat, we wanted to know, "What do we need to fix and how do we fix it?"

Improved technology was an obvious need. Four of the secretaries and several of the ministers did not even have access to computers. The office still functioned on typewriters. It was still common for ministers to dictate to shorthand-taking secretaries who then prepared typed copies.

We resolved to improve technology. Doing so, however, was not going to solve the problem. There were bigger issues at play. We began to ask management questions: Are we structured correctly to do the church's ministry? Are we doing the right things in the right ways? Do we have the right people in the right jobs?

Because we didn't have answers to those questions, someone proposed using an outside management consultant. Only one staff person expressed reservation by claiming that while outside consultants could be helpful, they also always recommended someone be fired.

That staff person's analysis was on target. We hired an outside management consultant. The consultant was enormously helpful. He provided a plan for reorganizing the staff to better serve the congregation's mission and ministry. As also predicted, the consultant identified one employee as a significant obstacle to church operations—the person who expressed reservation at hiring an outside consultant. With a different configuration of office personnel, less that person, things operated much more smoothly.

I was impressed by the management consultant and engaged him to teach the ministers how to better manage staff. He produced a notebook on Church Administration that was six inches thick. Topics ranged from The Art and Science of Strategic Planning to the latest business theories on Supervising, Managing and Motivating Others. It was an enormously helpful process that served me well, not only as a pastor in Kansas City, but as Seminary President in Lexington.

Being Criticized and Making Enemies
Comes with the Territory.

As a group, ministers like to be liked and love to be loved. We seek to make friends, not opponents. It is part of our nature. I don't think anyone enters ministry hoping to make enemies and be criticized. When a minister says, "I am following in the footsteps of Jesus," he or she has in mind the adoring crowd hanging on the Master's every word during the Sermon on the Mount, not the angry mob shouting epithets as Jesus dragged his cross toward Golgotha.

Fortunately, ministers receive significant amounts of positive feedback. To my knowledge, no other vocation has the equivalent of standing at the door after worship basking in the glow of weekly compliments. On the other hand, it is not possible to be liked by everyone, at all times, in every situation. Every faithful pastor will periodically be criticized and make enemies. It is never pleasant. One never grows accustomed to it. It just happens.

At the 4Cs, I came to realize criticism and enemies come in direct correlation to the size of the situation. The greater the responsibilities one has, the more difficult decisions one has to make. The greater the number of people being impacted by one's decisions, the more possibility there is for disagreement. This leads naturally to more criticism and more enemies.

The senior ministers of larger Disciple congregations were discussing this principle during dinner at an annual two-day retreat. Scott Colglazier, relatively new at a particularly large congregation, illustrated the point by referencing an eating utensil. *"If I move this fork from the left of my plate to the right, a group in the church will criticize me. If I place the fork on my plate, another group will be critical. If I leave the fork untouched, still another group objects. It doesn't matter what I do or don't do; someone is unhappy."* When Scott finished his little discourse, the remainder of the group nodded knowingly and whispered, *"Amen, brother. Preach it."*

Although I had experience with hearing criticism and making enemies in earlier pastorates, this became routine at the 4Cs. Sometimes people told me of their displeasure face to face. Sometimes I learned of their displeasure from the church gossip network. The anonymous letter was my least favorite method of learning someone was at odds with me. The Senior Minister of a large United Methodist Church in Texas once told me that before coming to that congregation he kept a file folder for anonymous letters. Now he had to have a four-drawer filing cabinet for anonymous letters.

Kansas City was much more congenial. One file drawer for anonymous letters was sufficient at the 4Cs.

Renewing the Congregation for the Future

Prior to coming to the 4Cs I was impressed that the congregation was roughly the same size in 1990 as it had been in 1950. Upon arrival I realized that was misleading. Demographically, this faith community was poised for significant decline. This was primarily due to the fact that the congregation had received 850 fewer new members in the 1980s than in the 1960s. The church had maintained its size by the same people growing older and older.

There is, of course, nothing inherently wrong with growing old. In fact, the more years I acquire, the more favorably I feel about aging. In terms of institutional maintenance, however, aging is self-limiting. At some point, a present generation must be replaced by the next generation. Toward that end, we were always working at the 4Cs on ways to reduce the congregation's average age. This included renewing worship so that it would be more attractive to younger adults.

The 4Cs, Kansas City

The Country Club Church equivalent of High Mass at Saint Peter's in Rome was the 11:00 Worship service. That service had a long-standing, well-deserved reputation for setting a standard of excellence in formal, traditional worship. The liturgy was of the highest caliber. The setting was architecturally magnificent. The music was outstanding. Consequently, it had an average attendance higher than the other two services combined. Unfortunately, the 11:00 also had an average age well past retirement. It was not attracting younger adults.

We set out to find ways to renew the service without either driving a wedge between the generations or destroying the service's reputation for excellence in traditional worship.

I believe we managed to do that, but it took a difficult process. Part of the problem was that nothing had changed in the 11:00 for three decades. When I arrived in 1991, the bulletin looked exactly as it had in 1961. It had the same picture on the front. The wording of the announcements about the flowers on the chancel was identical. Even the paper on which the bulletin was printed had not changed. I once threatened to redistribute a 1961 Sunday bulletin to see if anyone would notice.

We managed to refresh without substantially altering the order of worship. We made incremental changes. We began to recite the Lord's Prayer after the Call to Worship rather than after the Morning Prayer. We moved the Lord's Supper from prior to the sermon to after the sermon. We also offered more opportunity for the congregation to participate in the worship through readings and sung responses. After three years of experimenting and tweaking, our 11:00 service was slightly more attractive to a younger generation. For the most part, the congregation was pleased with the changes.

Of course, everyone was not happy. Even after tabulating the feedback from 1400 worship service survey forms, four elderly men took me for a two-hour lunch in order to register their displeasure. They wanted me to know the only thing that would make them happy was to change everything back to the way it had been.

From Wedding Mill to Marriage Ministry

The 4Cs had a long-standing reputation for doing weddings for non-members. The practice began early in the church's history when not everyone had a chance to be married in a church. Particularly those who had been divorced or wanted to marry outside their faith had difficulty arranging for a church wedding. The 4Cs had always been open to doing these special circumstance ceremonies. In fact, in the 1960s the church built a wedding chapel to serve this purpose. Consequently, it was common to perform 100-150 weddings annually. The vast majority of these weddings were for people who were not members at the 4Cs.

My predecessor had performed most weddings. Because I was not willing to devote almost every Saturday to weddings, I recruited the other ordained clergy to share the responsibility. It was not long before it became apparent that the 4Cs was little more than a wedding mill. We did little to prepare people for the marriage that was inevitably launched by the wedding.

In response to our collective discomfort, we invented a wedding and early marriage ministry called GREAT START. Succinctly stated, this was a program that combined PREPARE/ENRICH, an internationally recognized paper instrument that analyzed an engaged couple's relationship in a multitude of areas, and COUPLE COMMUNICATION, a series of workshops in which the participants are taught skills in communication and problem resolution. The effectiveness of this program quickly gained such a positive reputation that other ministers in Kansas City began to send couples to our GREAT START events.

Eventually we applied for and received a $200,000 grant from the Eli Lilly Endowment to take GREAT START nationally. Carla Aday and I did workshops around the country that trained other churches for this wedding and early marriage ministry. It also received attention from Public Television and was featured on a nationally televised Valentine's Day special.

One of the unexpected consequences of GREAT START is that some unchurched young couples began to join and become active at the 4Cs. In fact, weddings were a significant source of new young adult members. Prior to GREAT START, non-member couples seldom became church members.

For years, I had been observing to anyone willing to listen that, "Most people never get a lesson on how to how to be effective at the two most difficult tasks in life—being married and raising children."

When we had GREAT START up and running to help people with their marriages, we began to increase educational opportunities on parenting. Carla Aday headed this effort. On her first endeavor, she mailed postcards to a couple of thousand area households inviting the interested to come to the 4Cs for a light supper and lecture by a prominent local child psychologist. We had no idea what to expect, but over two hundred parents of small children came. Most had no previous connection to the 4Cs. Our message to them was that "this church cares about you and your children."

I have always thought it behooves a congregation to have a community service niche. That Country Club Christian Church specialized in wedding preparation, early marriage and parenting proved helpful in accomplishing the objective of reducing the average age of the congregation during my tenure.

A Capital Campaign to Renovate the Building and Expand Parking

Sometime during 1998, conversations began to percolate among leaders that we needed to address neglected capital needs, particularly:

(1) *Make the church's back entrance more welcoming.* In the previous two decades, the church's back alley door had become the only usable entrance for week day visitors as well as the main entrance for at least one-third of the Sunday morning worship attenders. The church needed a more welcoming back entrance.

(2) *Expand off-street parking.* For an average Sunday morning attendance of more than 800, the church had only 90 off-street parking places. Most people parked on neighborhood streets or on four of the six lanes of Ward Parkway. This arrangement worked well in the 1920s when Ward Parkway was a sleepy side street. By the 1990s it had become a major north/south connector. The church's use of Ward Parkway as a parking lot meant that Sunday morning traffic was choked to one lane in each direction. About six times each year, an unobservant motorist would plow into the rear of a church attender's parked car.

Fortunately, two houses adjoining the rear of the church's property came up for sale. A capital campaign would permit the 4Cs to buy those homes, tear them down and provide needed off–street parking. The extra parking would make Ward Parkway safer and neighboring streets less crowded. It seemed like a great idea.

(3) *Renovate the sanctuary.* Shortly after the close of the Second World War, the building underwent a major renovation. The three-story education wing was added, the magnificent stained glass windows were installed and the choir seating arrangement was changed. In the late 1990s the plan was to paint the sanctuary, replace the worn carpeting and return choir seating to its original plan.

The change to choir seating, more an afterthought than a priority, was intended to fix a design flaw. When the church was built in the 1920s, the choir sat facing the congregation. During the 1948 renovation, the planning committee opted for the fashionable design of the Post-War era. Instead of facing the congregation, the choir was divided with half of the singers on the right and half on the left with the communion table in the middle. The liturgical principle was that everyone in the sanctuary would face the Lord's Table, the center of Christian worship. The musical/sound theory was that each half of the choir would sing facing one another. The sound would mix in the middle and then somehow turn in the direction of the congregation.

While visually beautiful and vaguely reminiscent of the great European cathedrals of the Middle Ages, the design was acoustically flawed. Sound cannot be relied upon to make right-and/or left-hand turns in order to flow harmoniously over the congregation. For a half century the 4Cs music ministry had dealt with this design problem. The planning committee decided to improve the sound of the choir and restore the original chancel design. This also seemed like a great idea.

(4) *Find a home for the scupture.* Dominic Zappia was a Kansas City woodcarver. His *Magnum Opus* was a life-sized copy of DaVinci's "Last Supper." Jesus and the apostles were each carved from 300-pound blocks of basswood. The table is more than twenty feet long. The single-piece tablecloth shows how the cloth might have been folded before placed on the table. The sculpture was finished in time to be the centerpiece at the Protestant Pavilion during the 1964 New York World's Fair.

After the fair closed, plans for the sculpture's permanent home collapsed and two members of the 4Cs purchased and gifted it to the church. Unfortunately, the church had no place for the sculpture. It was just too big. For the next quarter century, Zappia's work was on loan to the Unity Church on the Plaza. They did an outstanding job exhibiting to the public. Thousands of people took advantage of the opportunity see it.

In the early 1990s, Unity Church leaders decided they needed the display space. We asked the world renowned Nelson-Atkins Art gallery to accept the Zappia sculpture into their collection. They said, "Thanks, but no thanks."

The sculpture was on temporary display at Rockhurst College, a local Jesuit institution, but problems developed. Fraternity boys regularly visited the display late at night to have their pictures taken while seated at the table with Jesus. The college's president assured me they had done no damage. As he explained, "They are just good Catholic boys who thought this was their best opportunity to sit at the Table with the Lord."

The upcoming capital campaign would give us an opportunity to resolve this issue. It was decided to use a Sunday School classroom on the main floor of the church to display this art object.

We presented this four-part case for capital needs and began fundraising. Our goal of approximately $2 million was oversubscribed in two weeks. With the excess we installed about $200,000 worth of long-needed lighting in the sanctuary.

In spite of a few difficulties mentioned in the next chapter, this was a successful endeavor. After these renovations, the facilities were much improved.

Busy, But Still Time for a Few Other Things

Serving as Senior Minister of Country Club Christian Church was physically, emotionally and spiritually demanding. It was not uncommon to have weeks in which I conducted four or five wedding rehearsals on Friday afternoon and evening before performing the weddings on Saturday. After getting home as late as 9:00 or 10:00 Saturday night, I got up at 6:00 a.m. on Sunday morning to prepare to preach at three worship services.

I began to write my sermon for the next week on Monday morning and completed it by Wednesday. Then I memorized the manuscripts on Thursday and Friday and practiced it aloud in the Sanctuary or Chapel a couple of times on Saturday. There were also meetings to attend with staff and congregational leaders, plans to formulate, people to see, Bible studies and other classes to prepare and conduct, books to read, letters to write, support staff to direct, ministers to evaluate and socials to attend.

December was the busiest month of the year. Each Advent Season meant more than twenty church-related Christmas socials. Although I enjoyed these events, there is a human limit to the number of evenings one can mill around, smile and chit-chat. I always looked forward to the last Advent social. Fortunately, the party season ended with awe-inspiring worship at the 4Cs Christmas Eve services at both 8:00 and 11:00 p.m. services. This always meant the magnificent sounds of the Kansas City Brass Ensemble and a full choir singing to packed houses at both hours. It was close to 1:00 a.m. Christmas morning before we returned to the parsonage and 2:00 a.m. before our sleep was deep and dreams were sweet. What a wonderful way to welcome the Christ Child!

Time was also squirreled away for my writing hobby. While in Kansas City I published three books of sermons, *Tenders of the Sacred Fires, Questions of Faith for Inquiring Believers* and *The Transforming Power of a Changed Perspective*. During a three-month sabbatical leave in the summer of 1998, a Lilly Endowment grant permitted me to study fifty large, mainline Protestant congregations that had renewed over long periods of time. That research led to the fourth book published that decade. It was on the principles of renewing mainline congregations and was entitled, *Dinosaur Heart Transplants*.

Writing and publishing while trying to manage pastoral duties may seem like a great deal of extra, even unnecessary work. One must remember, however, I did this for fun. It was my way to relax.

About two years after arriving in Kansas City, Colleen, our youngest daughter, graduated from physical therapy school. This marked the first time in twenty-seven years we were not raising children or paying school tuition. Budget-wise it was an enormous pay raise. We immediately spent the extra money on the mortgage for a 1,000 square foot A-Frame cottage on a tiny lake about fifty miles south of the 4Cs. In phonetic honor of the famed Kennedy Clan compound at *Hyannis Port*, we named our place the *Heiney Plop*. It was in Osawatomie, Kansas, where 140 years previously abolitionist John Brown came to national prominence by slaughtering a gaggle of slave-holding neighbors near the Kansas-Missouri border. The little place on Timber Lake served us well as a family get-away. I have fond memories of swimming, fishing, walking, running, talking and laughing with family and friends in Osawatomie. I still contend it ranks among the more beautiful places in the world.

A Very Special Honor

Early in 2000, Duane Cummins, President of Bethany College asked me to deliver that year's baccalaureate sermon during commencement weekend. He also said the school's trustees wanted to award me an honorary Doctor of Divinity degree for my distinguished ministry on behalf of the Christian Church (Disciples of Christ).

I had wonderful memories of being a student at Bethany, but I never thought the school would recognize me for my ministry. I was pleased. Larry Grimes, the school's most senior professor and a fellow freshman in 1960, read the tribute and commented that it took me forty years to get a degree—perhaps a record in the college's 160- year history.

Before receiving this degree, I often said, "An Honorary Doctorate is like a pig's tail. It tickles only the one to whom it is attached." Since June, 2000, I say, "I have two doctorates. One I earned (D.D., Bethany College). In order to receive the other (Doctor of Ministry, San Francisco, 1979), I had to take courses and write a research paper."

It's funny how circumstances can change one's opinion!

8

Marvels and Oddities: Ministry's Sideshow

A traveling circus has major and minor entertainment venues. The major acts are held in an extremely large tent called The Big Top. Typically hundreds, even thousands of people can be jammed onto bleachers to see acrobats, high-wire walkers and wild animal acts. The lesser venue is called The Sideshow. It is usually located on the midway near The Big Top. Housed in a series of smaller tents, each sideshow attraction accommodates only a couple of dozen paying customers to see out-of-the-ordinary wonders and curiosities like Fatima, The 800-Pound Lady; Terence Thumb, the World's Smallest Man; and Cashmere, The Two-Headed Goat. The Sideshow may be memorable, but it is not the main event. It is simply what happens on the way to the main event.

There is a sense in which ministry compares to the circus. Both offer main events and sideshow attractions. Ministry's main events include giving instruction on the meaning of faith, presenting hope in the midst of despair, offering comfort to the suffering and dying, helping people get in touch with God's love in Jesus Christ and pleading for God's justice.

Ministry's sideshow attractions are the peripheral marvels and oddities that happen on the way to what is important. The Capital Campaign at the 4Cs is an example. While outwardly a great success, it had elements of a sideshow. Recall the plan to renovate the sanctuary. A tiny portion of the campaign's funds were allocated to restore the original chancel design with the choir facing the congregation. Because the change would make a significant improvement in the sound of the church's music, it was assumed everyone would be in favor.

Unfortunately, many older members expressed their displeasure. Within a couple of weeks of announcing the sanctuary renovation, the planning committee received a petition with more than 200 signatures objecting to the plan. Ninety-six percent of the petitioners were over 65. The planning committee foolishly thought older people would love the change because it put things back to the way they used to be.

If the committee had researched the remodeling from fifty years previously, it would have discovered that the split chancel design had been the means by which the 1998 older generation had wrestled the reigns of leadership from the church's founding generation. The petitioners interpreted the proposed changes as an affront to them. "We put the sanctuary that way and now you want to change it. Who are you to change what we did?"

The lack of support from the older generation added stress to the campaign. I received many letters of protest—both signed and unsigned. The planning committee had a steady stream of older members demanding, begging and pleading that their wishes be observed. When individual efforts and a petition were not successful, they began calling other church members urging them not to contribute toward the campaign. When the fund-raising goal was subscribed within a few weeks, they hired their own architect to find a way to improve the choir's sound without significantly altering the 1948 configuration. Only having their architectural drawings unanimously rejected by the planning committee convinced them that they were not going to win the argument.

A Word about that Older Generation

By the late 1990s the young adults from 1948 were called America's Greatest Generation. This group, born between 1906 and 1926, survived the Great Depression and saved the world for democracy by defeating Imperial Japan and Nazi Germany. Upon returning from the war they led America in becoming the world's greatest economic, military and political power. In addition to supplying every President from John Kennedy to George H.W. Bush, America's Greatest Generation dominated local and state leadership positions for over a half century. They were leaders when they were young and they continued to lead into the last stages of their lives. There is good reason to call them America's Greatest Generation.

This generation's downside was their significant sense of entitlement. They had provided great leadership and believed the country owed them. In part because they did not think anyone could care for the world as well as they had, they were also slow to relinquish the reins of leadership. As might be expected, the older members of this generation became, the more tenacious they held on to leadership.

My entire career in congregational ministry was spent working with America's Greatest Generation. It was a joy when I was in my late twenties and they were in their early fifties. By the time I was in my late fifties and they were in their late seventies and eighties, it was a chore.

I decided that when I grew old I did not want to be one of those old men who insists, "In my life, I have seen thousands of changes and I have been against every one of them."

In addition to the chancel renovation, the neighbors' reaction to the church's plan to expand off-street parking became a major sideshow extravaganza. When the 4Cs announced plans to tear down two houses, the neighbors strenuously objected. Led by a handful of those living nearest the church, the Neighborhood Association brought a lawsuit. They also regularly picketed Sunday morning worship services after first alerting the local newspaper and television outlets.

Church leadership revisited the issue of whether or not adding off-street parking was essential and concluded it was. To remain a vital witness in this location, the congregation had to provide safe, off-street parking. A decision was made the fight the Neighborhood Association.

The Lawsuit Sideshow was long and expensive. I had been in Lexington for about one year when Carla Aday called to say the court found for the Neighborhood Association. When I heard that I said, "This day may be remembered as the beginning of the end for a strong Country Club Christian Church. The church has lost, but the neighborhood may well have lost as well." Ten years after that lawsuit, worship attendance at the 4Cs is declining. I suspect a part of the problem is that a younger generation is not attracted to a church that doesn't have a place for them to park.

A Marvelous Happening

During the fundraising phase of the capital needs campaign, a suggestion was made that we find one donor to give the estimated $80,000 for bringing the Zappia sculpture of the Last Supper into the church building. Toward that end, I wrote a column in the church's newsletter. Within a few days, a couple made an appointment to talk. They were in their early seventies and regular church attenders. It was a second marriage for each. His family was among the founders of the church. She had moved from New York City when they married. She had recently been diagnosed with cancer and the prognosis was not positive.

Their interest in the Zappia originated with the wife. When the sculpture was at the New York World's Fair, she was a young mother in an unhappy marriage. She often visited the fair in order to sit prayerfully in front of the Zappia. She claimed it was an enormous source of comfort. After her children were raised, she and her first husband divorced. She moved to Kansas City after marrying her present husband.

She was delighted to learn that the sculpture she loved in New York had been moved to Kansas City. When she discovered that the sculpture was owned by the church to which she belonged, she was even more delighted. As she put it, "That sculpture was meaningful to me during my first marriage, the unhappiest time in my life. It has been meaningful to me during my present marriage, the happiest time in my life. It remains meaningful as I approach my death. We want to fund bringing this sculpture into the church in hopes that others will find it meaningful into the future."

The couple concluded that they wanted their donation to be anonymous until after the wife's death. Then the church was to place a simple bronze plaque with their names as donors. The inscription was placed on the room shortly after her death. At the 4Cs All-Church Thanksgiving Dinner in 2010, I told the congregation this wonderful story.

A Representative Sampling of Notables Encountered Along the Way

One of the benefits of ministry is having the opportunity to brush shoulders with a scattering of prominent people. Some were nationally and internationally known. Others distinguished themselves without national or international recognition. Other than interesting, I claim no intrinsic value in having encountered them. My experiences were just part of ministry's sideshow.

GERALD FORD, *Minority Leader U.S. House of Representative, President of the United States,*

In the early spring 1968, Linda and I chaperoned thirty-five Michigan high school students on an International Affairs Seminar to New York City and Washington D.C. At the time, President Ford was Republican Leader of the House of Representatives and our Grand Rapids Congressman. I asked him to speak with our group about international affairs. He agreed and for over an hour he talked and fielded questions. When he finished he invited the entire group to the front steps of the Capitol for a group picture. For several years that photo of Bob, Linda, Gerald Ford and the youth group hung at the Gerald Ford Presidential Library in Grand Rapids, Michigan.

President Ford was a gracious, kind, considerate man.

ROBERT DOLE, *U.S. Senator from Kansas, Republican Nominee for Vice-President and for President*

I met Bob Dole on two occasions. Each time he was the evening speaker for a community-wide dinner and I was the designated pray-er. Senator Dole had a public reputation for being sharp tongued and ill tempered. In person, he was warm and witty. Linda's most vivid memory of Senator Dole is of having the seat next to him at a Chamber of Commerce dinner in Bedford, Indiana. The hard roll served to her crumbled on the tablecloth. She spent an embarrassing evening trying the keep the bread crumbs covered.

MARGARET THATCHER, *Prime Minister of Great Britain*

While in Kansas City, a couple in the 4Cs gifted me with a ticket to have lunch with the Prime Minister. Nicknamed The Iron Lady, she was one of the most engaging, most charismatic people I have ever encountered. She spoke to a small room of people for nearly an hour and kept us riveted by her presence as much as her message. After being with her, I understood why she is considered one of the most powerful women of the twentieth century.

ADLAI STEVENSON III, *U.S. Senator from Illinois*

Senator Stevenson came from a distinguished family of Illinois politicians. His great grandfather, Adlai I, was a U.S. Congressman and Vice-President in the second administration of Grover Cleveland. His father, Adlai II, was Governor of Illinois, twice the Democrat nominee for President and the American Ambassador to the United Nations. Adlai III was a U.S. Senator from Illinois and a twice-defeated candidate for Governor of Illinois.

I met Adlai III when he attended a family wedding in Bloomington, the hometown of his great-grandfather. I spent a wonderful evening chatting with him at the rehearsal dinner. At some point, I asked him how the Stevenson family became Democrats in a city with close ties to Abraham Lincoln and the Republicans.

He responded that family history research suggests the Stevensons of Bloomington were closet advocates for slavery. It seems even the most prominent families have skeletons in the closet.

JOHN ASHCROFT, *United States Senator from Missouri, Attorney General during President George W. Bush's Administration*

I met Attorney General Ashcroft when he came to a wedding at the 4Cs. I was a little uneasy at the news of his coming. According to press accounts at the time, he was so socially and personally conservative that he had ordered statues of nude women at the Department of Justice draped with white cloths.

I discovered he was really more of an Ozark Mountain Good-Old-Boy than a judgmental right-wing neoconservative. He had been raised in rural southern Missouri in a family of

Old-Fashioned Holy Ghost Pentecostals. I really enjoyed getting to know him. He was a jovial, warm human being.

JACK KEMP, *NFL all-pro quarterback, U.S. Representative from Buffalo, NY, Vice-Presidential Nominee*
I met Representative Kemp when he came to Bloomington to speak at the annual Chamber of Commerce dinner where I was the pray-er. He was the first person I heard advocate for supply-side economics, the cornerstone of conservative tax policy from the Reagan era forward. I was stunned that night when Kemp built the case for low taxes in the United States by citing how well Germany rebuilt following the total devastation of the Second World War by having a low tax rate. That comparison didn't make sense to me in 1985 and it still doesn't.

Kemp was a very nice fellow, but his gift was as a quarterback throwing a football to wide receivers, not as an economic theorist.

CLARENCE KELLEY, *Director of the FBI, served under Presidents Nixon, Ford and Carter.*
A native of Kansas City, Kelly was the city's Chief of Police when Nixon nominated and the Senate confirmed him as Director of the FBI. At that time, he was also an active member and elder at the 4Cs. Because his wife's health did not permit her to move to Washington, he returned to Kansas City and worship at the 4Cs regularly. On occasion, he would even lead the Children's Time at the 11:00 service.

When I knew him, age and the fog of Alzheimer's were increasingly problematic. I do, however, remember a few conversations in which he would be lucid for a few minutes and share stories about his time with the FBI.

His funeral was held at the 4Cs. It was attended by a host of dignitaries, including former FBI Director William Sessions whose father was a Kansas City Disciple minister. Director Sessions approached me in the church narthex, introduced himself and thanked the congregation by saying (to paraphrase): "This is like a great cathedral. Leaders could come from around the world to a State Funeral and feel welcomed."

Kelley's Memorial Service really felt like a State Funeral. The sanctuary was packed. More than a 100 local police stood at attention in the aisles. The city closed the freeway to other traffic as the funeral procession made its way to Kelley's Independence, Missouri gravesite. Footage from the Kelley funeral was on CNN that day.

There was one other service from the church's sanctuary that made the national news. In July, 1996, the 4Cs hosted one of four national Memorial Services for TWA Flight 800, a 747 jet that exploded and crashed 12 minutes after take-off from New York, killing 230 people. Because its international maintenance base was in the city, TWA chose Kansas City for a service. Hundreds of employees attended. Since the plane had recently been serviced in Kansas City, many expressed a concern that something they did might have contributed to the crash. Even after an intensive 14-month investigation, the cause of the crash remained uncertain.

LLOYD JOHN OGLIVIE, *Chaplain of the U.S. Senate.*

I met Chaplain Ogilvie when he came to the 4Cs as the guest preacher for our seventy-fifth anniversary observance. Before becoming Senate Chaplain, he had been a prominent Presbyterian pastor and preacher, author of 52 books and well-traveled lecturer. When he introduced himself in my office I was struck by two things: (1) He had a voice like God, only deeper; and (2) He was effervescent in telling me that when he was a Chicago seminarian, John Trefzger, one of my predecessors in Bloomington, had been his mentor.

When making arrangements for his visit, his office informed us that as Senate Chaplain, Rev. Oglivie was an ambassador to the American people and could not accept an honorarium. Instead, only travel expenses were to be reimbursed. In addition to a hotel and meals, there was to be a first-class plane ticket to accommodate Ogilvie's 6'6" frame. Furthermore, the church was expected to make a $2,000 gift to a charity of Ogilvie's choice.

In the end, the cost of our free-to-the-taxpayer speaker was over $3,000. It might be argued that this is a tidy sum for a Guest Preacher. In reality, that is not much money to pay for a warm memory and a good story.

DAWN UPSHAW, *Metropolitan Opera soprano, described by the Los Angeles Times as one of the most consequential performers of our time*

When I arrived in Bloomington in 1980, Dawn Upshaw was a student at Illinois Wesleyan University and a participant in the First Christian Church choir. The congregation paid her $5 weekly to lead the soprano section; $10 if she sang a solo. While in Kansas City, we contacted her New York agent to see if see if we could book her for a concert for the 4Cs seventy-fifth anniversary observance. When we were informed the standard cost for an evening was $50,000, it was decided to consider other entertainment.

A good story might be worth $3,000, but not $50,000.

HOWARD K. SMITH, *journalist and longtime network news anchor*

Howard K. Smith's career included such diverse activities as interviewing Nazis Adolf Hitler, Heinrich Himmler and Joseph Goebbels as well as moderating the first Presidential debates between Richard Nixon and John Kennedy. I met him a few years after he retired from ABC where he had been the anchor of the evening news for two decades. It was another of those Chamber of Commerce dinners where he was the speaker and I the pray-er.

As those to be seated at the head table were assembling for a grand entrance, I approached Smith and introduced myself. "I'm Bob Cueni, you probably recognize me. I am the fellow who always fell asleep when you were delivering the evening news on ABC."

Without a moment's hesitation, Smith looked in my eyes and replied. "Why, of course, I recognize you. I always wondered what your name was."

That night I learned never to try to outwit a national news anchor in a clever comment competition.

A Miscellany of Unforgettable Folks

During the course of ministry, one accumulates a large store of memories about ordinary, but very special people. In the grand scheme of things, none of this is really central to the faithful practice of ministry. These memories are part of ministry's sideshow. I wanted to record them before they are lost—like the foam trailing a ship.

WARD GEIB, an elder at the church, was our next-door neighbor when we first moved to Cascade. As a teenager, Ward thought about becoming a minister and even attended Johnson Bible College in Tennessee. The First World War intervened and he went off to fight the Kaiser. At the end of the war, he was one of several thousand American soldiers stationed in Russia as part of an unsuccessful attempt to stop the communists from taking over the country. After returning home, he married Elma. They spent much of their careers as custodial handyman and cook at First Methodist Church in Grand Rapids.

When I met him, Ward was in his early seventies and one of the most pleasant and energetic people I have ever known. He always had a clever comment to share with each person he met. He was a joy to be around.

Ward kept a notebook on those jokes, quips and bits of wisdom he so generously shared. Each time he heard or read something that caught his fancy, he wrote it down. When he needed new material, he consulted his notebook. He was not unlike this preacher who for years kept sermon illustrations on 3x5 cards in a small metal box.

While Ward never returned to complete his studies at Johnson Bible College, he had a very successful ministry of personhood. Everyone who knew him was enriched by the encounter.

LEWIS RUTHERFORD was a Springport, Indiana farmer and, like Ward Geib, a veteran of the First World War. For decades Lewis taught the older adult Sunday School class. A faithful churchman, his Sunday wardrobe consisted of a patterned flannel shirt, farmer styled bib overalls and a copy of the Tarbell Sunday School Guide twisted and stuffed into a rear pocket. Lewis was also a master at telling stories and offering poignant comments. With incredible verbal skill, he could take an otherwise insignificant incident or flash of memory and weave a tale or craft a one-liner.

He was not alone in having this skill. In fact, storytelling seemed a characteristic common to Indiana farmers. Perhaps this was a natural product of spending much of one's working time in solitude, at the steering wheel of large farm implements, plowing, planting, spraying and harvesting.

The business agenda of a Springport Church committee meeting usually lasted about ten minutes. The next hour was devoted to storytelling. Each farmer would offer a favorite tale while the others waited patiently for a turn. They were all master storytellers, but I liked Lewis Rutherford's tales the best.

On Paying Federal Income Tax. "Bob, when they passed that income tax thing in 1913, I decided I wasn't going pay it until somebody from the U.S. government came up on the back porch of my farmhouse and told me I had to. And I didn't.

"One day in 1922, I was sitting at my kitchen table having my lunch when this fellow in a suit came on the back porch and knocked on the door. When I answered he said, 'Mr. Rutherford, I am from the Internal Revenue Service and you haven't been paying your income tax.'

"I looked him in the eye and said, 'I know that. I have been waiting for you to stop by. Let me get my checkbook.'"

How to decide one's political affiliation. I asked Lewis how he had happened to become a Democrat when most Henry Country farmers were Republicans. He told me, "I noticed that when the Democrats were in office, I made money. When the Republicans were in office, I didn't."

Once one has served during time of war, further travel is not appealing. Lewis's son, a successful manufacturer's representative for farm equipment, was taking an extended tour of Europe. I asked Lewis if he had heard from him. He replied. "Yeah, he sent me one of those 'Wish You Were Here' postcards. I am not interested. In fact, if that Eiffel Tower was over behind my pig barn, I don't think I'd walk over to see it."

Enjoying a good memory. I happened to be in the Rutherford living room on the anniversary of the end of the First World War. At the time, Lewis was in his early 80s. I asked him if he was in the army on that first Armistice Day. A small smile curled from the corners of his lips as he pushed back and forth in his rocking chair and thought about that important day in American history.

"I remember it well," he said. "Four or five of us American doughboys were together, waiting for the end of the war.

We were holed up in a small chateau in the Argonne Forest with some French girls. We had been celebrating for three or four days— drinking wine, singing, having a good time, waiting for the war to end. The Armistice came on November 11 at 11:00—eleven, eleven, eleven. I'll never forget it."

The smile that had only curled from the corners of his lips grew to consume most of his face. He continued, "About 3:00 in the morning of November 12, the war was officially over and one of those French girls took off all her clothes and started dancing on the table." After a long pause, with eyes glazed by the memory, he said, "Bob, I believe that was the very best party I ever attended."

K.C. Festerling was an elder, adult Sunday School teacher and chair of the search committee that brought us to Petoskey in 1971. Karl Christian made his living advising people on how to solve problems in their homes and on their farms as the Emmet County Extension agent. K.C. had the energy level of a humming bird, the humor of a stand-up comic, the compassion of Mother Teresa and a remarkable ability to make and keep friends.

As might be expected, sometimes these qualities conflicted. For instance, there was a woman, let's call her Jane, who worked in K.C.'s office. When she was young, Jane's leg had been amputated and she wore a prosthesis. She and K.C. worked together for many years and were close friends. Apparently nothing, however, was out of bounds in their mutual and incessant needling. Jane constantly kidded K.C. about his bald head, and he regularly jabbered about her "wooden leg."

One day they were leaving the county court house on a snowy winter day. Jane slipped, tumbled down the long staircase and landed in a snow bank next to the sidewalk. Out of his great concern for his friend and colleague, K.C. raced down the steps to assist her. When he discovered she had not been injured, he was greatly relieved, but he could not let the moment pass without commenting, "Jane, I am so glad you weren't injured. I would not have known whether to get help from a doctor or a carpenter."

When K.C died suddenly of a heart attack within a few months of his retirement, I missed his presence. Ministry at First Christian, Petoskey was just not the same after he was gone.

GAIL BELL and I worked together for about six years as the pastors at First Christian Church in Bloomington. In addition to youth ministry, Gail assisted in nearly every other area of ministry. I have seldom met a man who had a more positive attitude. He radiated a sense of joy for life and ministry.

One of the other great things about having Gail on the staff was that he had an ability to develop personal relationships with people with whom I had little in common. For instance, he regularly invited the Cuenis to his men's group's Annual Skeet Shoot and Wild Game Cookout. This was not really my thing. I never hunt and thus had no wild game to contribute. Using disc-shaped clay projectiles for shotgun target practice was not something I longed to do. And, of course, I seldom have even felt tempted to cook squirrel stew over an open fire. In spite of that, I liked to go to this event because Gail gathered men who were his close friends, but only my nodding acquaintances. The Annual Skeet Shoot and Wild Game Cookout was a chance to know Gail's friends in their comfort zone.

Gail had grown up in rural Arkansas and the family had moved north to Michigan when he was a teenager. He had a delightful way of sharing stories from his hard scrabble beginnings.

"My grandmother," he would say, "had thirteen children. She told us, 'When I married your Granddad, he promised me the world. When the thirteenth child was born, I told him that was close enough.'"

"My mother grew up on a farm in Arkansas and she could cook anything—as long as it was fried."

"When I was kid in Arkansas, we had that fancy Sushi stuff they serve in better Japanese restaurants. We called it bait."

Gail was one of my favorite ministry colleagues. I both appreciated and loved him. A few years after I left Bloomington, he left to serve small congregations in Tennessee and Kentucky. Gail was retired and living in Clarksville, Tennessee, when he died. I was pleased to be asked to pay tribute to his life and ministry by delivering the eulogy. At the funeral, his son gave details about Gail's growing-up years that helped me better understand this man who had been so important to me. His Arkansas family were sharecroppers, e.g., the poorest of Arkansas' poor. In addition, the Bells had been migrant workers on the west coast of Michigan. As a child, Gail harvested cucumbers for pickles near Benton Harbor and picked cherries near Traverse City. When I was a public health employee, my heart had ached for the children who labored as migrants. Gail Bell, my beloved colleague in ministry, had been one of them.

HUGH WINNELL, a lifelong resident of Petoskey, was a faithful servant of the Christ and His Church. When I met him he was making his living as a barber. Eventually he became a successful insurance agent.

As most elders in the Christian Church (Disciples of Christ), Hugh had a phrase or two that he regularly repeated in his prayers at the communion table. My favorite of his was, "Oh Lord, we are as filthy rags." Hugh had a way with words.

Fortunately he understood that his words did not always convey the message he intended. In fact, he loved to tell of being the Master of Ceremonies at a church dinner honoring a departing pastor. "After everyone had eaten, I asked the women who had prepared the meal to come out of the kitchen so that we could express our appreciation. I wanted to say, 'Ladies, that dinner was *second to none.*' Instead, I said, 'Ladies that dinner was *next to nothing!*'

"No sooner had the laughter died down than I invited the minister to come to the podium. I intended to say, 'Reverend Hunter come up here and get your *farewell* gift.' Instead, I said, 'Come up here and get your *welfare* gift.'"

Hugh finished the story by saying, "The next day, Reverend Johnson from the Methodist Church came to my barber shop. I told him what I had done. He said he understood my embarrassment. He explained that once he was at the head table for a Methodist Bishop's retirement celebration. 'As the least distinguished person at the head table,' he said, 'I was the last to speak. When my turn came, my prepared remarks had all been used. As I walked to the podium I had to mentally revise my flattering comments. Off the top of my head, I told the crowd that since coming to Michigan, this Bishop has been the backbone of our conference ministry. In fact, he has been the very bottom of the backbone.'"

Hugh died in August 2012. He was nearly ninety. They said the last week of this life he told anyone who would listen: "I can't wait to shake the hand of Jesus."

Hugh still had a way with words.

SECRET SANTA was the name the Kansas City *Star* gave the otherwise anonymous man who appeared each December to give cash, typically in $100 bills, to needy people. The newspaper usually had an annual article about a beneficiary of this man's generosity. "He just walked up to me on the street and gave me money for Christmas," was a typical comment.

In the middle 1990s, Linda and I were invited to a dinner party at the home of Dr. and Mrs. Rich Davis. Rich was a Kansas City child psychiatrist and member of the 4Cs who had made it big by selling a backyard grilling concoction he called, K.C. Masterpiece Barbecue Sauce.

There were both strangers and members of the congregation at the dinner table. When Rich made the introductions, he told us that one of the guests, Larry Stewart, had given permission to reveal that he was the Secret Santa of Kansas City. When someone asked the obvious questions, Larry said that each year he gave away about $50,000 and that his generosity was motivated by childhood memories of the Salvation Army delivering Christmas baskets to his house.

In 2006, after he was diagnosed with terminal esophageal cancer, Larry Stewart revealed his identity to the newspaper. It is estimated that he gave away about $1.3 million in his lifetime. He died in 2007 at age 58.

DON AND JOAN GRAY have been friends for decades. I met Don in fourth grade. Linda does not remember a time in her life when she did not know him. Don was best man at our wedding. I was a groomsman at the Gray's wedding. Each summer for more than twenty-five years, the Grays and the Cuenis have vacationed together.

In our time together, we really don't do anything out of the ordinary. We laugh. We talk. We go out to dinner together. Don and I play golf. Linda and Joan go shopping. Hours are often spent reading silently in the same room.

Everyone needs friends. Friends are the people who help us survive. Don and Joan are our friends. There is no better way to explain why we so value our time with the Grays.

Obviously, this only a sampling of the wonderful people we have met in ministry. There is simply not enough space in a single volume to mention them all. However, the opportunity to encounter so many wonderful people has been one of the greatest blessings of ministry.

9

Life as a Seminary President

Sometime in the early to middle 1990s, Richard Dickinson, the President of Christian Theological Seminary, invited me to join the Board of Trustees at my Alma Mater. I accepted his invitation. Seminary had been a meaningful experience, and I looked forward to being a part of making it meaningful for the next generation of ministers.

I served a term or two on that board and learned a great deal about theological education. When Dr. Dickinson retired, I was even nominated to replace him as President. I cannot remember exactly how that happened, but I got as far as an interview before they chose another person. When I finished my time on the CTS board of trustees I assumed my contribution to theological education had ended.

In the early summer of 2001, I received a phone call from Tobie Vandervorm, a recruiter for Academic Search in Washington D.C. She was staffing the search for the next President of Lexington Theological Seminary and said I had been nominated.

When Tobie asked if I would agree to have my name forwarded to the search committee, I queried, "Why would they consider me? I am not an academic. I do not have a PhD. My only experience in theological education is as a student, a member of a Board of Trustees and teacher of an occasional course." I concluded with another question, "What are they looking for in their President?"

She responded by recounting events of the previous spring. The LTS President, Rick Harrison, had resigned to become a local church pastor. Almost simultaneously to Rick's resignation, Tony Dunnavant, the school's 40-something Dean, died unexpectedly after cancer surgery. As if the losses of the President and Dean were not sufficient, the faculty was in disarray. Four professors had come up for a tenure vote at the same meeting. At LTS, granting tenure was usually a routine matter. Anyone not meeting faculty expectations was normally gone before an actual vote in the sixth year. In this instance, that had not happened and two of the four professors were rejected for tenure.

Tobie continued by saying that the turmoil swirling over the Dean, the President, and the faculty had divided the student body and alumna/ae. Because both dismissed professors were well-known Disciples, the issue was generating a negative reaction from the denomination. The entire situation was becoming an issue among donors. Morale within the seminary community and across its constituency groups was low. She concluded, "You also asked what LTS needs in a new President. They need someone who can help heal relationships, rebuild the school's sense of community and get the seminary moving in the right direction."

I thought about it and responded, "I may not have any particular experience in higher education administration, but LTS seems to need the skills I have. Go ahead and submit my name." That set in motion my move from a career in the very familiar world of pastoral ministry to a sojourn in the unfamiliar territory of theological education.

Called From as well as Called To.

Before deciding to make a change in ministry sites, it is always a good idea to prayerfully ponder if and how God might be involved in the decision. By experience, reason and faith, I have come to believe that if there are not good reasons for being called from a present ministry as well as called to a new ministry, God is probably not in it and relocating is likely not a good idea. Unfortunately, it is not always easy to discern the presence and call of God. Responding faithfully is seldom, if ever, an exact science.

That said, I did have a sense of certainty about being called away from Country Club Christian Church and pastoral ministry as well as being called to a ministry in theological education at Lexington Theological Seminary. I felt called away from the 4Cs because I was becoming increasingly aware my effectiveness had passed its zenith. Serving as the senior minister at the 4Cs was physically, emotionally and spiritually demanding. As a younger man I had no trouble working 10- to 14-hour days, seven days a week. In fact, I was energized by it. As I approached the seventh decade of life, I noticed my energy beginning to decline. The normal process of aging was making itself known.

I suppose I could have adjusted by altering my labor- intensive approach to pastoral ministry by cutting back on commitments and working fewer hours. I did not think that was either realistic for the church or an attractive personal option. To flourish, the 4Cs needed a pro-active, energetic senior minister. The job could not be done by someone gliding toward the golden years.

Additionally, I have never understood how to do pastoral ministry in fewer hours or with less effort. Actually I never sought an easier way. When no longer capable of doing the job the way I thought it needed to be done, I planned to do something else. Before that phone call from Tobie Vandervorm, it had begun to dawn on me that I was starting to run out of gas in pastoral ministry. I was open to being called away from Kansas City and pastoral ministry.

As the process began to unfold, I also sensed a blossoming call to Lexington Theological Seminary. The stated needs of the school matched my gifts and skills. I was also at an age when leaving a legacy was becoming important. A seminary presidency would give me an opportunity to make a difference into the future by helping to form the next generation of ministers. The more I thought about it, the more my sense of call to and away from was confirmed.

The LTS Context for Ministry and Administration

Throughout the 1990s, the United States had a long run of peace and prosperity. The stock markets soared. Jobs were plentiful. Economically those were good times. By the late 1990s, the federal government was more than financially healthy. The country began to use its budget surplus to pay down the national debt. Internationally our traditional nemesis, the Soviet Union, collapsed. The United States found itself dancing alone on the world stage as the only super power. America gushed prosperity, self-confidence and optimism.

The financial situation of the Seminary was not as positive late in the summer of 2001 when I interviewed. The search committee explained that Kentucky Fried Chicken's Colonel Sanders had once dependably provided about half of the school's annual fund. After his death, the Colonel's foundation continued to give generously, albeit at a lesser amount. A few years before my arrival, the attorneys for that foundation moved the money to Canada and stopped all contributions. The loss of fifty percent of LTS's annual fund over a few short years significantly stressed finances. The school had a previous history of drawing too heavily on its endowment. To make up the loss of the Sanders money, LTS began to use even more money from the endowment. Whereas the higher education standard is four or five percent, trustees told me they thought the LTS draw was closer to eight percent.

Of course, the nation's economic good times could not last forever. As that fellow who knocked himself out throwing big rocks into the air and walking under them confirmed, "What goes up must come down." By September 2002, a year after the terrorist attacks of 9-11 and six months after I began at LTS, the Dow had lost almost forty percent of its value. The NASDQ had lost a significantly higher percentage. LTS's endowment, which supplied most of the money to run the school, lost about forty percent of its value. The endowment decline necessitated an even higher percentage annual draw, perhaps as much as eleven or twelve percent.

Getting Started

The trustees understood that this new president did not have experience in seminary administration. To help with what we all knew was going to be a steep learning curve, Harry Richart, the chair of the search committee, and Carlean Hefner, chair of the trustees, told me to take the first month of my employment to prepare for the transition from pastoral ministry to higher education leadership. They recommended reading widely on what seminary presidents do, talking to people who had transitioned from senior minister of a large congregation to seminary president and preparing a plan for what needed done in the first few months on the job.

What a magnificent gift. The entire month of March 2002 was spent working on those recommendations. I communicated with congregational ministers turned seminary presidents; read all that was available on seminary presidency; and visited former LTS Presidents Hal Watkins, Wayne Bell, Bill Paulsell and Rick Harrison. I studied the Seminary's constitution and by-laws, the faculty and staff handbooks as well as several years of board and faculty meeting minutes.

The trustees' gift of that month gave me time to develop an action plan for dealing with the aftermath of the previous year's battle over tenure. When I got into the office I immediately began resolving conflicts, rebuilding relationships and restoring trust not only among faculty and staff, but with other Seminary stakeholders.

Within a year or so, significant progress had been made in changing the atmosphere within the school. The back-biting and angry confrontations that had been reported as regular occurrences lessened significantly. Of course, everyone did not live happily ever after. Academic institutions are by nature contentious places. Simply being church-related did not make the Seminary an exception. Outwardly, however, the halls, classrooms and offices became more peaceful—at least for a few years.

Simultaneous to work on relationship building, I also pulled together ideas to knit into a vision for guiding LTS into the future. At my inauguration as fifteenth President of LTS on August 31, 2002, I announced that Lexington Theological Seminary should strive to be *"The leading Disciple seminary where those God calls into ministry are shaped as exceedingly faithful, highly effective leaders of the Church of Jesus Christ; and that will be done in a way that is distinctively Disciples, inherently ecumenical, and academically excellent."*

In that inaugural address I listed what I thought was needed to move toward realizing that vision. Among other things, I said the entire Seminary will need to: (1) Recruit significantly more students with great potential for ministry. (2) Maintain an ecumenical presence. (3) Increase our financial base by significant additions to the present cadre of committed givers. As President, I presented this as the Seminary's map to the future.

Unfortunately, the Map is Not the Territory

In the Bicentennial summer, our family drove from northern Michigan to San Francisco so that I could do coursework on a Doctor of Ministry degree. Our transportation was a 1973 Chrysler that seldom got more than eleven miles to the gallon. Inside the car we carried a AAA TripTik®. This handy reference guide provided mile-by-mile directions as well as suggestions for near-by American Automobile Association-approved motels and restaurants.

While purchasing gas in Buffalo, Wyoming, I turned the TripTik® page to the next stretch of road. It did not differ particularly from previous pages. It was a highlighted black line drawn on a mostly white page. I noticed the line seemed to have more turns than usual and that the altitude changed significantly in the road ahead. The Auto Club narrative indicated our family was about to cross the Big Horn Range of the Rocky Mountains.

I knew the Rockies were somewhere west of Chicago. I had heard stories and seen pictures. I had never actually driven in the Rockies, but how bad could it be? The map shows the road as just another crooked black line across a white page.

An hour or two after leaving Buffalo, we arrived in Ten Sleep, Wyoming, population 300. Linda had spent much her time stretched out on the front seat with her face covered so that she could not see the sheer mountain drop-offs at the edge of the road. The girls sat silently in the back seat, their usual chatter stilled. During this mountain sojourn, my slight fear of heights escalated to near paralyzing terror. I experienced an important truth that day: maps do not fully reflect the reality of the territory.

My roadmap to LTS's future and the Auto Club map from Buffalo to Ten Sleep had the same critical flaw. Both described some, but not all the facts. Maps, after all, never picture reality perfectly.

When I interviewed for the job, the Presidential Search Committee was forthright in describing problems of declining student enrollment and inadequate funding. The committee members assured me they thought these could be fixed in a reasonable amount of time.

Although I am convinced they sincerely believed that, I am not as certain they were fully aware of all the factors that hampered student recruitment and financing the Seminary. These issues complicated living into the projected vision.

The Challenge to being inherently ecumenical

At my inauguration, I insisted LTS "cannot be Disciple without being ecumenical. This is part of our nature, our DNA." This call for an ecumenical student body was not new. For decades United Church of Christ, Presbyterian, United Methodist, Unitarian Universalist, Episcopal, middle of the road Baptists and other Protestant students matriculated at LTS.

Late in the twentieth century, the Lexington Diocese of the Roman Catholic Church began to contribute to our ecumenical mix. The Seminary began to offer two Master's degrees for Catholic laity. By the time I arrived, Roman Catholics studying to be parish administrators and directors of Christian Education comprised a significant portion of the student body.

The school's rich ecumenical footprint began to change when a new Episcopal Bishop began to require all Lexington Diocese seminarians to attend Episcopal schools. His explanation was understandable. A person is formed as an Episcopal priest by the practice of spiritual disciplines. In an Episcopal Seminary students attend worship and prayer services multiple times each day. As a typical non-Episcopal Seminary, LTS does not do that. Consequently, we lost our Episcopal students.

Early in 2004, an application was submitted to renew our status as an approved seminary of the United Methodist Church. In the halls of LTS this was considered a pro-forma matter. We had been graduating Methodists for at least sixty years. There had never been a problem with re-approval.

Imagine the shock when we received a letter saying that we could no longer educate United Methodist students. The stated reason was that LTS did not have a proper United Methodist ethos. We responded that there could not be much wrong with our UMC ethos since a Bishop in Georgia, the number two person in the New York City office of United Methodist ecumenical affairs, all the most recently appointed Kentucky District Superintendents and a host of Kentucky pastors were United Methodist graduates of Lexington Seminary.

We tried for a year to regain our approved status, but were not successful. LTS lost access to all students from the largest Mainline Protestant Church in America—the United Methodists.

About my fourth year, a new Bishop was appointed to the Lexington Diocese of the Roman Catholic Church. He seemed a great choice. A canon lawyer by training, he was a warm, charming man with a reputation for ecumenical cooperation. When I talked with him about financial support for the Catholic program at LTS, he was very supportive. He even attended the first fundraising reception for Catholic donors and was effusive in praise of LTS and its Roman Catholic Master's programs.

The morning after that fundraiser, the Bishop publically announced that according to his reading of canon law, only men ordained as priests and deacons were permitted to be parish administrators and Christian Education directors. Every non-ordained person serving in one of those positions had to be replaced.

This effectively ended our Catholic studies program. About 90 percent of our Catholic students were women wanting to serve in and for their church. There was little incentive for a woman to prepare for a career from which she was automatically excluded.

The lack of Episcopal, United Methodist and Roman Catholic students posed a serious roadblock to the vision of being inherently ecumenical.

Consequences of a Declining Christian Church (Disciples of Christ)

For more than four decades, our little branch of the faith has been declining. Each year, several thousand members of our churches are lost and a few dozen congregations close. In addition, there are fewer dollars given each year to national and international ministries of the Disciples.

I was both aware of and lamented those trends. As a local church pastor, however, I had no particular experience with the consequences of the decline. The congregations I served were generally healthy and usually growing. That changed when I came to a church-related institution that relied heavily on the denomination for students and money.

My first insight into how Disciples decline hampered living into the vision of being the leading Disciples Seminary came when I discovered that in the 1970s over forty percent of the Seminary's budget came from the Disciples central mission fund. By the end of the twentieth century that percentage had declined to less than four percent and was continuing to fall.

About the same time, I did a longitudinal study on seminarians. It revealed that over the previous twenty-five years, there had been a fifty percent decrease in Disciples studying for the basic ministry degree. That helped explain why LTS was having trouble recruiting Disciples students.

It was going to be extremely difficult to be the leading Disciples Seminary when we could not rely on the Christian Church (Disciples of Christ) either for adequate funding or a sufficient pool of potential students.

Correcting for the Excessive Draw on the Endowment

When I first arrived, the Business Manager told me that it would require taking $250,000 less each year from the endowment to reduce the draw to the higher education standard of five percent. Making up that difference did not seem an impossible task. With careful cost cutting and some increased giving to the school's annual fund I thought we could be out of this hole in a couple of years. At meetings with the Dean, Business Manager and Development team, I began to repeat the London, England subway mantra to "Mind the Gap." These words warn subway riders of the dangers of standing too close to the edge of the platform. I used Mind the Gap to caution Seminary leadership to be careful about the distance between the school's income and expenses.

Unfortunately, the Seminary Budget Gap was much larger than the initially reported quarter-million dollars per year. The amount doubled to $500,000 when the Business Manager included salary and benefits to replace faculty and support staff from the recent unpleasantness. A year or so later, I learned a $250,000 revenue item in the budget assumed to come from an outside funding source was actually an additional annual endowment draw. Negative information continued to trickle out of the business office until The Gap started to resemble The Chasm.

Eventually it became clear that attaining a five percent draw was going to require taking at least a million dollars less from the endowment each year. My simple plan to resolve the school's financial problem by careful cost cutting and some increased giving to the annual fund was not realistic. The Seminary budget was too far out of balance. Instead of minding a small gap, we really needed to fill a financial Grand Canyon.

In six-plus years at the Seminary we constantly dealt with the excessive draw on the endowment. Although our efforts resulted in some improvement, we never resolved it. For that matter, we never found a way to recruit a critical mass of students either.

Lexington Theological Seminary

Benefits and Satisfactions of Being President

Lexington Theological Seminary has a long and distinguished history. Founded in 1865, it is the oldest continuing Disciple institution devoted exclusively to preparing church leaders. In addition to being one of the founding schools of ATS, the accrediting agency of theological education, LTS lays claim to being the nation's first seminary to have specialized professors in Pastoral Care and Religious Education.

LTS also has a longstanding reputation for preparing highly effective pastors for local congregations. In fact, my ministry followed in the steps of ministers formed by LTS. Late in the nineteenth century, George Hamilton Combs, the organizing minister of Country Club Christian Church in Kansas City, received his pastoral instruction at Kentucky University, the earliest name for LTS. Early in the twentieth century, Edgar DeWitt Jones, the Bloomington pastor for whom the pulpit is dedicated, matriculated at the College of the Bible, another early name. In the mid-twentieth century, John Trefzger, the Indiana pastor who submitted my name at Bloomington, graduated from the school a few years before the name changed to Lexington Theological Seminary.

For nearly one and a half centuries, under three different names, LTS has contributed mightily to the mission and ministry of the Church of Jesus Christ. To have served as LTS's fifteenth president was an honor and privilege. Being President also provided experiences of deep satisfaction.

The Joy of Fundraising

Asking people to give money is central to any seminary president's job description. Fundraising involves activities as diverse as writing letters, making phone calls, visiting donors, holding fundraising events and giving leadership to telethons. Presenting the case for why people might want to give is also a necessary part of fundraising. At LTS that meant attending regional assemblies and gatherings of Disciple ministers, speaking and doing workshops in a variety of venues, building relationships with potential donors as well as preaching in Disciple churches throughout the Southeast United States.

Although some seminary presidents claim to dislike fundraising, I rather enjoyed it. Three and a half decades of congregational annual fund drives taught me that asking for money is integral to ministry. At LTS another lesson from the local church was confirmed: generous people are also very nice folks. For that reason, building relationships with donors is an enormously pleasant activity. It was a joy to meet and spend time with alumna/ae, current and former trustees as well as other donors.

Of course there was even more joy when people made significant gifts. I was particularly pleased to be instrumental in the Seminary receiving two of the larger gifts in its history—the $1.2 million given for the Donald and Lillian Nunnelly Teaching Chair in Pastoral Leadership and the $500,000 gift from Blanche and Luther Coggin to enhance the education of ministers. There is great joy in fundraising.

The Joy of Associating with Faculty

Outside the halls of higher education much is made of the difficulty of working with faculty. The rap is that as a group, the faculty will always be uncooperative with the administration and that individually every member of the faculty has a gift for being argumentative. That, of course, is an unfair generalization. On occasion the faculty will cooperate fully with the administration and there are faculty members who have no particular talent for being argumentative.

Personally, I found that while there were some frustrations in working with faculty, there was joy in associating with faculty. They are incredibly intelligent, significantly disciplined folks with interesting life experiences. This leads to enlightening and delightful conversations. One of my favorite memories is of overhearing two faculty members discussing a mutual acquaintance—the Vatican archivist responsible for translating documents into Medieval Ecclesiastical Latin. That very conservative academic refuses to permit modern terms to creep into his translations. He always finds ancient terms for modern things.

These two LTS faculty members began to wonder aloud how the archivist might translate *minivan*. After discussing several possibilities from their own knowledge of Medieval Latin, they decided *minivan* would be translated with the Latin for *small chariot*. Associating with faculty can be fun.

The Joy of Working with Students

The opportunity to work with students was one of the chief attractions of going to LTS. I thought I would enjoy helping form the next generation of ministers. I was not disappointed.

I taught courses, preached sermons in chapel and had regular conversations with ministry students. I loved telling stories from the pastorate and talking about the lessons learned along the way. Of course, I don't know how much influence I had or did not have. All ministry is that way, including a seminary presidency.

Gary Straub, a friend and colleague, compares ministry to bowling through a heavy drape. You roll the ball down the alley. It passes under the curtain. You hear the ball crashing into pins. However, you do not see what actually happens. Only when a postcard arrives in the mail some days later do you learn your score. Ministry is comparable. It may take years or even decades before one learns the impact of a ministry. Fortunately, I have started to get some of those postcards from my time at LTS. Consider this sampling:

A former student wrote me a letter of thanks. At his graduation I had advised him to accept a call from a congregation that would challenge him rather than one that would be within his comfort zone. He followed that advice and has made it a guiding principle for ministry.

A highly effective pastor took my class in church administration and expresses her appreciation every time I see her. In fact, she quotes from my lectures.

Linda and I endowed an annual award for the best preacher in the graduating class. A winner of that award pulled me aside at graduation to explain she first became excited about preaching when she heard me preach in chapel. She claimed to have been so deeply moved by my sermon that she decided "I want to learn to preach like that."

There was a student who entered LTS as what might be characterized a "bright, well-intentioned fellow with significant potential for ministry but a paucity of social graces." He matured enormously during his studies, served an internship in a major Disciple congregation and is now a highly effective pastor. Recently the newspaper in the town where he serves ran an article on the difference this young man's ministry is making in their community. What a blessing to be even an observer of a student coming to realize his or her potential in ministry.

The Joy of Travel

Before coming to LTS I seldom traveled in the Southeastern United States. For instance, my experience of Alabama and Georgia had been limited to driving through on the way to New Orleans and Miami. I had never even visited Northern Mississippi or Eastern North Carolina. I was totally uninformed of the beauty of Florida's panhandle seacoast and Maryland's countryside. I had never delighted in different accents of Virginians, Georgians, Carolinians and Alabamians. I was even clueless to the rich variety of Southern barbeque.

The time spent as LTS President corrected for this shocking experiential deficiency. The culture, customs, geography, language, people and Disciple congregations of the Southeast became very familiar. Ascending this learning curve was a never-ending source of delight.

Improved marital communication was a totally unexpected benefit of LTS travel. The terrorist attacks of 9-11 increased security at airports and made flying inconvenient as well as uncomfortable. I began to drive to places where I might otherwise have flown. That made it economically feasible for Linda to become an unofficial ambassador-at-large for LTS by frequently accompanying me. This resulted in Linda and I spending a large portion of many days together, behind the windshield, freed from the distractions of daily routine. The last time we spent that much time in uninterrupted conversation we were teenage friends chatting across the kitchen table. It was a wonderful opportunity to review our fifty-year relationship as well as plan for the future. That time together was a wonderful blessing. In fact, we believe our near seamless transition to retirement was facilitated by those trips on behalf of LTS.

Down the Homestretch

Even though pleased with improvements in LTS finances, I knew they were inadequate. The incremental changes we implemented would take fifty years to produce the needed result. We needed a paradigmatic shift in the Seminary's way of being and doing. We needed something significant to happen from the outside.

Possibilities were even imagined and investigated. One seminary had a wealthy entrepreneur who almost singlehandedly funded their financial transformation. Maybe LTS could find a person like that. Another seminary's financial problem was corrected by a large foundation. Maybe there was some group that would help LTS.

When I was unable to locate an entrepreneur or foundation, I began to admit the only meaningful alternative was to drastically change the way LTS functioned. I thought, with a stable stock market, the school had a window of about five years to accomplish this.

By then I was nearly sixty-six years of age. The prospect of working another five years was not particularly attractive. For that matter, I was not sure I had a great idea of how Lexington Seminary should look in the future. Consequently, in January 2008, I announced my retirement pending the call of a new President.

Facing My Own Finitude
The death of Craig Witte about that time contributed to my decision to plan for retirement. Linda and I met Craig and Dorothy Witte when they started attending the Bloomington church about 1982. They became personal friends. We had many happy times eating at area restaurants, attending University of Illinois football and basketball games and spending holidays together. Craig accompanied me when I went to visit Karen in Kenya. The four of us even spent a delightful week in a condo on Central Park South while visiting New York City. It was a memorable friendship. After their divorce in the early 2000s we did not have as much contact. Craig and I, however, continued to exchange an occasional email or phone call.

One day, Craig's brother called to say Craig was hospitalized with severe breathing problems and might benefit from a phone call. Over the next two weeks I called frequently. Craig's father had died of a lung disorder and apparently Craig had the same illness; unfortunately, with the same result. We returned to Bloomington for Craig's funeral. I delivered the eulogy.

My friend's death discombobulated me by confronting me with the inevitability of death. Craig died and I was going to die. I didn't

know when, where or under what circumstances, but it was going
to happen. I had many things planned for retirement. I had better
prepare to do them.

On April 21, 2008, I delivered my final report to the board
of trustees. It was entitled: "LTS: Its ministry and mission into
the twenty-first century." I opened that report by saying that
"The head of the Association of Theological Schools contends
one-third of all seminaries are significantly stressed, typically by
lack of students and/or money. He says these schools can flourish into the future only if they make significant changes in the
way they recruit students and raise funds, as well as manage
their assets and educational processes.

"LTS falls into this group. This great, historic school is caught
in a series of very significant trends in the church, society and
theological education that make it difficult both to recruit a
critical mass of students and adequately fund the school's operations.

"I characterize our situation this way: We are traveling
north on Interstate 75. The trip is going quite well. We have
gas in the tank. The vehicle is greased, oiled and running on
all cylinders. We are making good time and almost without exception, people seem to be enjoying the journey. The problem
is that Chicago is our destination and Interstate 75 doesn't go
to Chicago. No matter how well things are going at the present moment, LTS needs to get off the road we are on and get
on one that will take us into a future where the Seminary can
flourish in its mission and ministry."

On the occasion of my retirement, the Trustees threw a
grand soiree at the University of Kentucky's Spindletop Hall.
Guests included a multitude of friends and colleagues as well as
our daughters, sons-in-law and grandchildren. Several attendees honored my ministry with kind comments. Even though
much of the praise ranged from exaggerated to pure fabrica-
tion, I loved hearing it anyway. It was a wonderful celebration.

I officially left office on September 1, 2008, when Jim Johnson began as the sixteenth president. The first ten days of the
next month, the stock market declined by 18.1 percent. For the
year, the Dow lost 33.8 percent of its value. It was the stock

market's third worse year since its founding in 1896. Unfortunately, the Dow Jones decline was just part of a wider economic downturn with serious problems in banking, investment and housing sectors. The nation's sudden and unexpected economic downturn profoundly impacted the Seminary. The five-year window of opportunity projected for a paradigmatic change in LTS operations had been telescoped into months.

Much to their credit, in a very short period of time, the new president and board of trustees led the Seminary into the sea change it needed. Today, Lexington is primarily an on-line seminary with students enrolled from across the country. The curriculum permits students to remain close to home and is based in congregations rather than seminary classrooms. The budget is greatly reduced. The draw on the endowment is near the goal of five percent. Only time will tell if these changes work long-term. However, I am both impressed and thankful for the leadership of others during that critical time. As for me, I headed off to retirement.

10

Retirement as Visiting the County Fair

As in many small communities, the week of the county fair was Petoskey's busiest of the summer. For six consecutive days from 10:00 a.m. until 10:00 p.m., thousands crowded the fairgrounds to walk the midway, wander the agriculture exhibitions and meander over to see who won this year's Blue Ribbons for biggest pig, tastiest parsnip and crispiest canned sweet pickles.

Twenty years before the Cuenis arrived, someone at First Christian Church saw the Emmet County Fair as a fundraising opportunity. "We could open a food booth to sell hamburgers, coffee and soft drinks. The profits will help pay the loan for the new building. It will be fun!" Thus began a church activity that would annually involve a majority of church members.

Over the years, the menu grew to include, among other things, homemade pie and potato salad—fifty freshly baked pies and one hundred pounds of potato salad per day. By the time the Cuenis arrived in Petoskey, operating a food booth at the county fair was a tradition almost as unbreakable as the Sunday observance of the Lord's Supper.

As church pastor I not only enjoyed the food and fellowship at First Christian's fair booth, I found great satisfaction in the Emmet County Fair itself. I loved to wander the midway and the exhibitions for no other purpose than to be amazed. "Look at all of this activity," I would think to myself, "and I did not have to do one thing to make any of it happen! I did not attend any committee meetings, do any planning, recruit any volunteers or solve any problems. Others took full responsibility. What a wonderful blessing not to be in charge."

Retirement has been a little like attending the county fair every day of every year. I have moved from being a Decider in my immediate surroundings to being a Spectator. Whereas I once worried that I would not be content in retirement, I have found that I love not being in charge. Someone once described this experience as "the deep joy that comes by finally realizing you are not responsible to keep the stars spangled in the heavens and the earth turning on its axis."

In retirement my days are filled with activities of my choosing: studying Spanish, wandering through the family genealogy, reading books for personal enjoyment, keeping faith with my ordination vows and writing these memoirs.

Spanish began as a lark and has become a passion. When asked why I spend about two hours each day studying I usually reply, "Eventually I may move to a nursing home where the caregivers are likely to be Spanish speaking. To communicate if I *need* to go to the bathroom or I have *already been* to the bathroom, correct Spanish verb tenses will be necessary. At that stage of life nothing will be more important." A more honest answer is that I enjoy it. In addition to providing the capacity to chitchat with servers in Mexican restaurants, studying a foreign language keeps the mind sharp.

For thirty years there has been an old family Bible on my bookshelf. On the flyleaves are recorded the travels of its owner, my paternal great-great grandfather, a Union soldier during the Civil War. One of the more intriguing entries notes, "A.H. Cole was in Lexington, Kentucky on April 28, 1862." Particularly after moving to Kentucky, I wanted to know more about this man. What was he like? What was he doing in Lexington?

In retirement I have had time to research not only the life of A.H. Cole but other family members. Even though what I do falls short of the demands of careful genealogical research, it has proven to be a delightful way to investigate the twists, turns and oddities in our clan's history.

This genealogical sojourn seems to raise as many questions as it answers. For instance, I have wondered: Was Irish immigrant Owen Fee satisfied with his new life as a farmhand in western New York? What prompted A. H. Cole to desert the Union Army on Christmas Day, 1862? Why did the birth parents of my stepfather purchase land in their native Hungary in 1913, then leave for the United States a few months later?

Unfortunately, there are no available records to answer those questions. At least I have never been able find notes tucked into family Bibles, caches of personal letters or published memoirs. I assume there were once family members who could have answered these queries, but those tenders of family lore have died. With their passing the answers to my questions have been lost.

For decades, reading was part of my ministry. I preached nearly every Sunday and needed a continual supply of sermon ideas and illustrations. A delightful benefit of retirement has been the opportunity to read widely for no other purpose than I find it interesting.

Because one can never fully retire from the vows of ordination, I have continued a few activities related to ministry. To sustain some form of spiritual discipline, we attend worship and Sunday School almost as regularly as we ever have. To remain aware of the concerns of the least among us, I assist Linda in distributing food to the poor at God's Pantry, a local food bank. I wrote and published a book of sermons, *When Walls Shift and the Ceiling Collapses* (CSS Publishing, 2012).

In addition, I have done brief interim ministries in Bethany, West Virginia, and Kingwood, Texas. These were accepted for both personal and professional reasons. My year at Bethany College in 1960-61 was a highlight of my early adult life. An interim at the college church gave me an opportunity to see whether or not the community was as idyllic as I had remembered. (It wasn't. No present day reality could match the idealized memories of my year at Bethany College.) Because our youngest grandson attends the Kingwood Christian Church that interim ministry opportunity was irresistible. (Being near Karen, Karl and Bryce Tillett surpassed all expectations.)

Time: The Gift of Retirement

In the busyness of previous decades I was so involved doing ministry and living daily that there was not sufficient time to ponder the order of my life, how things fit together and what it has meant. Retirement has given me an opportunity for extended reflection. To illustrate, I have always felt blessed by my marriage and my children. In the course of writing this memoir I have taken the time to think about what it takes to parent a child and to be meaningfully married.

On Raising Children: When Linda came home from the hospital with Karen, we laid our eldest down for her first nap in a newly painted, secondhand bassinet. We spent a moment basking in the aura of, "Wow, look what we did. She is beautiful!" Then it dawned on us that we had no idea what to do when she awakened from that nap. For all intents and purposes, we were clueless about parenting.

Fortunately, by trial and error; a heavy reliance on God's grace; wearing out a couple copies of Dr. Benjamin Spock's paperback, *Baby and Child Care*; regularly seeking guidance from those with experience as parents; and applying lessons from a course called "Parent Effectiveness Training," we not only figured it out, but I believe we can rightly claim some success. Our daughters are wonderfully mature women, mothers, wives, employees and citizens. Reflecting from the eighth decade of my life, I believe we stumbled on some sound principles of parenting. Here are five.

(1) Start with a healthy baby. It is best for a child to be not only healthy as an infant, but as free of potential future health problems as possible. Obviously this is beyond the parents' control, but there's no denying that a child with a healthy body, an untroubled mind and a set of uncluttered genes significantly facilitates effective parenting. A person can, of course, do an outstanding job raising a child with a birth defect or a genetic predisposition for a physical, emotional, learning or behavioral disorder. However, those complications make parenting much more difficult.

We were fortunate. Karen and Colleen were born healthy. Other than standard prenatal care, we did nothing to ensure their health. Our children's worst potential disorders were the genes for shortness and sweaty feet. Providence, not good parenting, needs to be credited.

(2) Give time to your children. Encourage them. Talk with them. Listen to them. If you show no particular interest in what is going on in their lives when they are four and the issues are trivial, they will not likely be open to conversation when they are in their teens and the issues are potentially serious.

(3) Introduce your children to responsibility and account-ability from the time they are small. Start with little things. Work up to big things. Permit them to make age-appropriate decisions.

Unless they could be seriously harmed, don't rescue your children either from unpleasant circumstances resulting from the inherent unfairness of the universe or from the consequences of their decisions. Give them advice, guidance and encouragement, but let them learn how to cope with their problems and make their own decisions.

Let me illustrate this principle. Colleen and Karen were nine and twelve years of age when Linda introduced them to living on a budget. Every six months, each girl was credited with a certain amount of money. Since they were not old enough to safely handle that much cash, the girls maintained notebooks on their income and expenditures. Each was empowered to decide purchases of clothing, shoes and haircuts. During the first six months of this plan, one of the girls bought more expensive shoes than she could afford and ran out of money. Consequently she did not have funds to buy summer clothes. Over-spending never happened again. In fact, after a year or so, both Karen and Colleen maintained positive balances in their accounts. Today both our daughters teach courses on personal finance in their churches.

(4) Jettison any notion that as a parent you can control everything in your children's lives. Despite a parent's best efforts, children encounter failure, experience outside negative influences, stumble into undeserved problems as well as misery of their own making. That is the nature of this world. Children are not formed in the controlled environments of laboratories. They are human beings coming of age in an inherently capricious world. All a parent can do is his or her best. Then we must let go of schemes to control and rely on God's Grace.

(5) Even as Scripture assures us that there is nothing that can separate us from the love of God, we need to assure our children that there is nothing that can separate them from the love of their parents. In spite of bad grades and inappropriate behavior, through indecisiveness and poor decisions, whether a success or a failure, good parenting anticipates standing by our children. They need to know that even if we don't approve of their decisions or behavior, they can count on our unconditional love.

On Being Married. On our wedding day, Linda and I may have known less about marriage than we did about parenting on the day Karen was born. Over the past half century, we have learned a great deal. I offer a sampling of five lessons.

(1) Understand that good marriages are made, not discovered. Linda and I have more than a good marriage. We have what might be called a relational synergy that permits each of us to be more and do more because of our relationship that we could ever do or be without our marriage. This synergy did not grow naturally from our serendipitous meeting when we were children. It happened because we have been committed to work on our marriage through the decades. The love that holds us together has been created together. It has been hammered out on the anvil of daily give and take, offering forgiveness and being forgiven, sharing and receiving.

We have continued to build on the quality of our marriage by striving to know, understand and thus to behave toward each other in ways that are mutually satisfying. In other words, we try to behave as though we understand "If Mama is not happy, nobody is happy and if Daddy is not happy, nobody is happy." When we were young, practicing mutual satisfaction was hard work. Now that we are old, it is still hard work—albeit not as hard.

(2) Strive to remain friends. Before we fell romantically in love, Linda and I were friends. We liked each other. We enjoyed talking. We were kind to each other. We valued the opinions of each other. We treated each other as mutually treasured children of God. In addition to being lovers, parents and helpmates, we have continued to be friends.

This includes applying the standards for friendship to marriage. For instance, in the midst of a marital dispute, I am sometimes tempted to say something I know will crush my opponent
and give me a victory. Before I do, I try to remind myself, "I
can't say that. Linda is my friend. I would never say something
like that to a friend." Being friends facilitates a relationship.

(3) Deal with the fact that human beings continue to change
through the life cycle. Linda and my needs and circumstances
at nineteen and twenty were very different than when we were
in our forties. They are also different now that we are retired.

Over the years, we have adjusted continually. Knowing
what I know now, at our wedding, we should have vowed, "I
love you now and I will strive to love who you become." This
requires remaining open for negotiation and renegotiation.

The universality of continual change negates any notion
that two people could find happiness by getting married "just to
see if it will work." A healthy relationship requires the on-going
commitment to do what needs done to make it work.

(4) Learn to live with the less than perfect. Even though it
is important not to let problems in a relationship fester, don't
fall into the trap of thinking every problem can and should be
solved. It cannot be done. We are imperfect people living in
an imperfect world. At its best marriage is a joy to experience,
not a problem to solve. To put that a bit differently, remember
that the most happily married people are the ones who accept
they are not going to be happy about everything nor will they
always be happy.

(5) Make friends outside the marriage and family. It is un-
necessarily difficult for two people to carry the burdens of marriage and family alone. Get involved in a wider, caring faith
community with friends of shared values and experiences. We
have found that being part of the church does this very well.

A Final Reflection on the Next Phase of Life

Many people accomplish their best work at ages well into
their supernumerary years. Although God could have that in
mind for me, I do not anticipate it. In part because I had no
leftover ministry agenda, I am surprisingly content not having
a paying job. For more than forty years, I battled boredom.

I lived with the continual restlessness of wondering what to do next. When I was the President or the Senior Minister I willingly shouldered the burdens of responsibility and account-ability. Others regularly sought my opinion. I expected to have input. I might have, on occasion, even had fleeting thoughts of indispensability.

I now better understand and accept that others are quite capable. I not only <u>can</u> let others take charge, I really <u>must</u> do that. Rather than limiting, it is liberating to step aside and let others assume their turn. It is supposed to be that way. I once read a physician's contention that it is a blessing for an older generation to step aside. As a scientist, he claimed new genera-tions are in the best interest of our species and the continuity of humankind's progress. In his own way, poet Lord Alfred Tenny-son agreed with the man of science. "Old men must die or the world would grow moldy, would only breed the past again." If asked, I suspect Tennyson would agree his observation applies to women as well as men.

We live in a world where the inevitability of death and the changing of generations are God's natural order. Of course, as a Christian I do not see this as hopelessness. There is more to life than being born, growing up, growing old, dying and being re-placed by the next generation. I believe that this God who loves us in life does not abandon us at the moment of our death. In Christ, there is life, death, and then Resurrection to Eternal Life.

I do not profess to know the details of Eternal Life. How-ever a rabbi friend once shared a helpful image from medieval Jewish mysticism. To paraphrase, he said, imagine the world is only an ocean. That means, of course, there are waves. By definition waves are part of the ocean before they come into being and while they are waves. When waves cease to be they go back into the ocean.

The rabbi went on to compare that ocean to God, the ground of our being out of which we all come. Each wave might be thought a person. In this imagery, our lives are com-parable to coming into being and having our opportunity in the sun before returning again to the ocean. This resonates with the teaching that life is eternal. It is without beginning and without end. Like the water within the ocean that forms the waves and then returns to the ocean, we come from God and we return to God.

With that imagery, I came out of the ocean of God in 1942. My wave has been journeying for seventy years, the biblical standard for a full lifespan. At the threescore and ten year mark I am in good health. Perhaps I will make it to fourscore. I might even make it to fourscore and ten. As with most people I would like to come to end of this life with a clear mind, minimum decrepitude, manageable pain and adequate funding. In that way, I could avoid being a burden for others.

That it has passed too quickly is my only complaint. The comedian Mel Brooks is said to have observed, "When I was about 21 years old I stopped one morning for coffee and a bagel. I got to talking with friends and when I came out of the bagel shop I was old enough to retire. I don't know where my life went."

I know of what he speaks. It does not seem possible that Linda and I have been married for a half century. I know that our daughters are in their early and mid-forties but it seems not much more than a decade ago we were preparing for their births and only a couple years ago they went off to college. Life has moved swiftly.

Yet it also needs said that my life has been carried on a billowing cloud of God's grace. The disappointments have been few and the regrets almost nonexistent. The sum of my failures is well within established human norms. I believe I have grown through and learned from every difficult circumstance encountered. I have been more loved than I deserved and have had the opportunity to love others. I have known joy and believe I have brought a modicum of joy to others. There is not much more one can ask of life. I have been richly blessed.

When that day comes when I am called to change my membership to the Church Triumphant, I shall say farewell with Indiana poet James Whitcomb Riley's

A PARTING GUEST
What delightful hosts are they —
Life and Love!
Lingering I turn away,

This late hour, yet glad enough
They have not withheld from me
Their high hospitality.
So, with face lit with delight
And all gratitude I stay
Yet to press their hands and say,
"Thanks.—So fine a time! Good night."

9 781603 500319